CONTENTS

HOW TO USE THIS RESOURCE

Welcome to *Disciples Path: The Journey*. In Volume 3 you'll continue to explore biblical stories of disciple-making and replication in order to gain a better understanding of what it means to follow Christ. As you get started, consider the following guides and suggestions for making the most of this experience.

GROUP DISCUSSION

Because the process of discipleship always involves at least two people—the leader and the disciple— each session of *Disciples Path: The Journey* includes a practical plan for group engagement and discussion.

This plan includes the following steps:

- **GET STARTED.** The first section of the group material helps you ease into the discussion by starting on common ground. You'll begin by reflecting on the previous session and your recent experiences as a disciple. After spending time in prayer, you'll find a practical illustration to help you launch into the main topic of the current session.

- **THE STORY.** While using *Disciples Path: The Journey*, you'll find opportunities to engage the Bible through both story and teaching. That's why the group time for each session features two main sections: **Know the Story** and **Unpack the Story. Know the Story** introduces a biblical text and includes follow-up questions for brief discussion. It's recommended that your group encounter the biblical text by reading it out loud. **Unpack the Story** includes practical teaching material and discussion questions—both designed to help you engage the truths contained in the biblical text. To make the most of your experience, use the provided material as a launching point for deeper conversation. As you read through the teaching material and engage the questions as a group, be thinking of how the truths you're exploring will impact your everyday life.

- **ENGAGE.** The group portion of each session ends with an activity designed to help you practice the biblical principles introduced in **Know the Story** and more fully explored in **Unpack the Story.** This part of the group time often appeals to different learning styles and will push you to engage the text at a personal level.

✛ DISCIPLES PATH.

THE JOURNEY
VOLUME 3

LifeWay Press®
Nashville, Tennessee

DISCIPLES PATH

Disciples Path is a series of studies founded on Jesus' model of discipleship. Created by experienced disciple makers across the nation, it offers an intentional pathway for transformational discipleship and a way to help followers of Christ move from new disciples to mature disciple makers. Each study in the series is built on the principles of modeling, practicing, and multiplying:

- Leaders model the life of a biblical disciple.

- Disciples follow and practice from the leader.

- Disciples become disciple makers and multiply through the *Disciples Path*.

Each study in the series has been written and approved by disciple makers for small groups and one-on-one settings.

MINISTRY GRID®
training made simple

For helps on how to use *Disciples Path,* tips on how to better lead groups, or additional ideas for leading this study, visit: *ministrygrid.com/web/disciplespath*

Item: 005790760 • ISBN: 978-1-4300-6325-4

Eric Geiger
Vice President, LifeWay Resources

Sam O'Neal, Joel Polk
Content Editors

Michael Kelley
Director, Groups Publishing

We believe that the Bible has God for its author; salvation for its end; and truth, without any mixture of error, for its matter and that all Scripture is totally true and trustworthy. To review LifeWay's doctrinal guideline, visit *lifeway.com/doctrinalguideline.*

Unless otherwise indicated, all Scripture quotations are taken from the Christian Standard Bible®, Copyright 2017 by Holman Bible Publishers. Used by permission. Scripture quotations marked (ESV) are from The Holy Bible, English Standard Version® (ESV®), copyright © 2001 by Crossway, a publishing ministry of Good News Publishers. Used by permission. All rights reserved. Scripture quotations marked (NIV) are taken from the Holy Bible, New International Version®, NIV®. Copyright 1973, 1978, 1984, 2011 by Biblica, Inc.® Used by permission of Zondervan. All rights reserved worldwide. *www.zondervan.com* The "NIV" and "New International Version" are trademarks registered in the United States Patent and Trademark Office by Biblica, Inc.®

To order additional copies of this resource, write to LifeWay Resources Customer Service; One LifeWay Plaza; Nashville, TN 37234-0113; fax 615.251.5933; call toll free 800.458.2772; order online at *lifeway.com;* email *orderentry@lifeway.com;* or visit the LifeWay Christian Store serving you.

Printed in the United States of America

Groups Ministry Publishing; LifeWay Resources
One LifeWay Plaza; Nashville, TN 37234-0152

INDIVIDUAL DISCOVERY

Each session of *Disciples Path: The Journey* also includes content for individual use during the time between group gatherings. This content is divided into three categories:

⬆ **Worship:** features content for worship and devotion. These activities provide opportunities for you to connect with God in meaningful ways and deepen your relationship with Him.

➡⬅ **Personal study:** features content for personal study. These pages help you gain a deeper understanding of the truths and principles explored during the group discussion.

⬅➡ **Application:** features content for practical application. These suggestions help you take action based on the information you've learned and your encounters with God.

Note: Aside from the **Reading Plan,** the content provided in the Individual Discovery portion of each session should be considered optional. You'll get the most out of your personal study by working with your group leader to create a personalized discipleship plan using the **Weekly Activities** checklist included in each session.

ADDITIONAL SUGGESTIONS

- You'll be best prepared for each group discussion or mentoring conversation if you read the session material beforehand. A serious read will serve you most effectively, but skimming the **Get Started** and **The Story** sections will also be helpful if time is limited.

- The deeper you're willing to engage in the group discussions and individual discovery each session, the more you'll benefit from those experiences. Don't hold back, and don't be afraid to ask questions whenever necessary.

- As you explore the **Engage** portion of each session, you'll have the chance to practice different activities and spiritual disciplines. Take advantage of the chance to observe others during the group time—and to ask questions—so that you'll be prepared to incorporate these activities into your private spiritual life as well.

IMMERSED IN THE WORD

Immersing ourselves in God's Word provides
the foundation for our identity and life.

REFLECT

Welcome to Volume 3 of *Disciples Path*. The goal of this resource is to help you explore the process of growing and maturing as a disciple of Jesus. Throughout the following pages, we'll examine how disciples of Jesus imitate Him by immersing themselves in God's Word, remaining connected to God through prayer, and living in community with other believers. You'll also gain a deeper understanding of your mission as a follower of Jesus who lives, works, and plays in a world that's often opposed to Him.

In this session, we'll begin by discovering Jesus' approach to Scripture as God's Holy Word and practical steps we can take to imitate Him in this activity.

Which element in the description above are you most excited about? Why?

How can a better understanding of spiritual disciplines strengthen our relationship with God and increase our ability to participate in His redemptive purposes in the world?

PRAY

Begin the session by connecting with God through prayer. Use the following guidelines as you speak with Him:

- Ask God to open your hearts and minds to hear what He has to say through His Word today.

- Thank God for His Word, which is described as perfect, restorative, trustworthy, wise, right, clear, insightful, pure, sweet, and helpful.

- Ask God for wisdom and understanding as you seek to gain a deeper understanding of God's Word.

INTRODUCTION

Who is Jesus? Do a quick Internet search and you'll find many different answers. Some of those answers will be quite specific, while others will leave you with more questions than answers. Regardless, you're bound to land on some controversy and disagreement.

Perhaps a better way to answer this question is to go to God's Holy Word. Scripture, from the beginning of Genesis to the end of Revelation, points to Jesus. Simply put, the Bible is about Jesus. It's not about us and what we must do—it's about Jesus and what He has already done. And while it is crucial for Christ-followers to read the Bible, *how* we read the Bible may be even more important. John Calvin says this about reading God's Word:

> The Scriptures should be read with the aim of finding Christ in them. Whoever turns aside from this object, even though he wears himself out all his life in learning, he will never reach the knowledge of the truth.[1]

When we find Christ in Scripture we will know better how to be His followers. We will be able to communicate with Him and know who He is. And though the Bible isn't about us, we will begin to understand who we are in relation to Christ. In God's Word we find that we are both more broken than we dare let on and more loved than we dare let in. In God's Word, we find our true identities, the most authentic version of ourselves. It's only when we immerse our entire lives in God's Word that we begin to live the lives God designed and desires for us.

What have you heard others say is the primary reason to read the Bible?

How does this description of the Bible differentiate it from other books throughout history?

During this session, we will explore how we can be saturated and immersed in God's Word in a way that transforms how we see God, ourselves, and the world around us.

KNOW THE STORY

After Jesus' resurrection, Luke 24 describes the story of two disciples traveling to Emmaus. On their way, a man joined them. Unbeknown to them, this man was Jesus Himself. He asked the disciples about their conversation, and they told Him how they were troubled with Jesus' death and the news that His tomb was empty. Jesus responded in verse 25,

> 25 He said to them, "How foolish and slow you are to believe all that the prophets have spoken! 26 Wasn't it necessary for the Messiah to suffer these things and enter into his glory?" 27 Then beginning with Moses and all the Prophets, he interpreted for them the things concerning himself in all the Scriptures.
> LUKE 24:25-27

As they continued on their journey, Jesus reminded them of the Old Testament Scriptures and prophecies that revealed all that would happen. Jesus told the confused disciples that all of Scripture was revealing who He was. They had no reason to be troubled because He was who He said He was and accomplished what God had sent Him to accomplish.

A few verses later in the same chapter, Jesus then presented Himself before all of the confused and troubled disciples. And in the same way, Jesus encouraged them by saying,

> 44 He told them, "These are my words that I spoke to you while I was still with you—that everything written about me in the Law of Moses, the Prophets, and the Psalms must be fulfilled." 45 Then he opened their minds to understand the Scriptures. 46 He also said to them, "This is what is written: The Messiah would suffer and rise from the dead the third day, 47 and repentance for forgiveness of sins would be proclaimed in his name to all the nations, beginning at Jerusalem. 48 You are witnesses of these things. 49 And look, I am sending you what my Father promised. As for you, stay in the city until you are empowered from on high."
> LUKE 24:44-49

What are some truths we can take away from these two passages?

UNPACK THE STORY

SCRIPTURE REVEALS JESUS

He taught them how to understand Scripture and how all of redemptive history is pieced together and culminated at the cross. In verse 27, we read that "beginning with Moses and all the Prophets, he interpreted for them the things concerning himself in all the Scriptures" (Luke 24:27). Jesus used the Scripture to give these disciples hope in the resurrection. Jesus had previously told them that He would die and be resurrected. When He presented Himself to the disciples, He revealed that all He had taught them had come true. Jesus of Nazareth is the Lord Christ—the Son of God.

Jesus is recorded quoting Scripture 78 times in the New Testament.

Discuss some of the events in the few days surrounding Jesus' death and resurrection. What was it that made the disciples lose hope and doubt what Jesus had taught them?

When are you most likely to lose hope or doubt what Scripture teaches? Discuss how being immersed in Scripture turns that doubt into hope.

This wasn't the first time Jesus used Scripture. In Luke 4, as Jesus was fasting in the wilderness for 40 days, He was tempted by God's enemy, Satan. Of the three recorded temptations, Satan attacked Jesus' identity and began two of them with "If you are the Son of God ..." (vv. 3,9). Satan essentially dared Jesus to prove His identity by doing something amazing: turning stones to bread and jumping off the temple so the angels would catch Him. Because Jesus had immersed Himself in Scripture, He didn't have to prove His identity to Satan. Instead, He countered each temptation with the truth of Scripture.

We see this all throughout the Gospels. Jesus knew Scripture. Even as a young boy, He learned it. He memorized it. He meditated on it. And then as an adult, He allowed it to influence His ministry in countless ways. Jesus is recorded quoting Scripture 78 times in the New Testament.

Read Psalm 119:9-16 out loud in your group. How would it affect believers' lives who meditated and hid God's Word in their hearts on a daily basis?

SCRIPTURE REVEALS WHO WE REALLY ARE

Even though all of Scripture points to Jesus—and we read it with the intention and expectation of finding Jesus in Scripture—it doesn't mean we can't find anything useful in Scripture concerning ourselves. The opposite is true. When we immerse our lives in God's Word—through faith in the living Word that is Jesus and through immersing our lives in the written Word that is the Bible—we find an unshakable identity from which our entire lives can flow. Look at how these passages describe the Scripture's usefulness in the believer's life:

> [16] All Scripture is inspired by God and is profitable for teaching, for rebuking, for correcting, for training in righteousness, [17] so that the man of God may be complete, equipped for every good work.
> 2 TIMOTHY 3:16-17

> For the word of God is living and effective and sharper than any double-edged sword, penetrating as far as the separation of soul and spirit, joints and marrow. It is able to judge the thoughts and intentions of the heart.
> HEBREWS 4:12

What do these verses tell you about how God's Word shapes us?

Just as all of Scripture points to the cross of Jesus and the identification of Him as God's Son and the coming Messiah, we too can find and embrace a new identity when we immerse ourselves in God's Word. When we read the Bible with the expectation of finding Jesus, we'll begin to see that through faith in Him and His works we are adopted into God's family as His children and are given new identities. Sadly, we often forget this truth and have to be reminded of it daily. If we're not memorizing and meditating on God's Word on a consistent basis, we cannot expect to fend off Satan's attacks. The more we study God's Word, the more we learn about our identities and what God expects from us as His children.

The more we study God's Word, the more we learn about our new identities and what God expects from us as His children.

What are some challenges believers face when they read the Bible? Discuss some ways they can overcome these challenges?

ENGAGE

Charles Spurgeon, a well-known preacher from the 19th century, once said: "As the rain soaks into the ground, so pray the Lord to let His gospel soak into your soul."[2] It is the repetitive pounding of the moisture into the earth that transforms it from a parched, dusty, hard ground to rich, moist, useful soil. When God's Word saturates into our thirsty souls, we will experience transformation.

Perhaps a better metaphor would be one that happens in the kitchen. Consider how meat is often saturated (sometimes for hours) in a marinade so that it will be more tender and flavorful. With that imagery in mind, consider what it would be like to saturate your entire life in God's Word in such a way that it transforms you from ordinary to extraordinary, much like a piece of meat gets completely transformed after it has been saturated in a great marinade.

In your last few minutes together, spend some time discussing ways that someone's life can be transformed by immersing himself or herself in Scripture. If there are specific passages or personal stories that come to mind be sure to share those with the group. This exercise will help you see the variety of ways in which the Bible speaks and hopefully inspires believers to delve more fully into His Word.

PRAYER REQUESTS

....

....

....

....

....

....

....

....

....

....

....

....

1. John Calvin, *The Gospel According to John 1–10* (Grand Rapids: Wm. B. Eerdmans Publishing, Co., 1961), 139.
2. Charles Spurgeon, as quoted at *spurgeononline.com*. Accessed April 29, 2015.

In addition to studying God's Word, work with your group leader to create a plan for personal study, worship, and application between now and the next session. Select from the following optional activities to match your personal preferences and available time.

⬆ Worship

☑ Read your Bible. Complete the reading plan on page 14.

☐ Spend time with God by engaging the devotional experience on page 15.

➡ ⬅ Personal Study

☐ Read and interact with "Marinade Instructions" on page 16.

☐ Read and interact with "The Transforming Power of Scripture" on page 18.

⬅ ➡ Application

☐ Memorize Hebrews 4:12: "For the word of God is living and effective and sharper than any double-edged sword, penetrating as far as the separation of soul and spirit, joints and marrow. It is able to judge the thoughts and intentions of the heart."

☐ Spend time journaling. Just as Jesus countered each of Satan's temptations by quoting Scripture, Jesus often turned to God's Word as the authority for His life. Journal about a time when God's Word spoke to you and you did something differently as a result. What happened? How did it impact your perception of Scripture?

☐ Share with others. Take time to contact a few people this week with encouragements from Scripture. This could be people within your group or those outside your group that you sense need an encouraging word.

☐ Other:

⬆ WORSHIP

READING PLAN

Read through the following Scripture passages this week. Use the space provided to record your thoughts and responses.

Day 1
2 Timothy 3:10-17

Day 2
Psalm 19:1-14

Day 3
Joshua 1:1-9

Day 4
1 Corinthians 15:1-11

Day 5
Psalm 119:89-112

Day 6
1 Peter 1:13-25

Day 7
Deuteronomy 6:1-9

IMMERSE YOURSELF IN GOD'S WORD

Perhaps you are wondering: *How do I immerse myself in God's Word? What does that look like day-to-day?* This week find a verse that you want to soak in and get to know. If you don't have one on the top of your mind, use one from the daily reading plan on the previous page. Follow the steps below and answer all the questions before your group meets again.

Your passage: _____

Memorize and Know Scripture

Write this passage from memory below.

How would you explain this passage in your own words?

Meditate and Believe Scripture

What does this passage say is true about God?

What does this passage say is true about you?

Exercise and Apply Scripture

How are you believing or not believing in the truth of this passage?

How can you show someone else the truth of this passage?

PERSONAL STUDY 1

MARINADE INSTRUCTIONS

For marinade, or God's Word for that matter, to completely saturate something, or someone, there are four things that need to happen. We need to get in, get under, get through, and get transformed.

Get In: Just like an item needs to get into the marinade and be completely soaked, we've got to get into Scripture. First, once we begin a relationship with Jesus, we receive God's Spirit who enables us to understand Scripture in a way we never could before (see 1 Cor. 2:14-15). Second, when we grasp that the story of God revealed in Scripture spans from eternity past to eternity future, we begin to understand that our lives are actually a storyline within God's Story. We find the context for who we are as we begin to let God narrate and shape our existence through His Word. Finally, over time, we will actually begin to get into Scripture like we do a great book or movie. We actually look forward to it. We desire it!

> *Have you ever thought about your life being a storyline within God's story? How does that make you feel?*

> *What are typically the biggest distractions from you getting in the Word and allowing God to be the narrator of your life?*

Every story about God's people throughout Scripture is a story about your spiritual family tree. If you are a Christian you have been adopted into God's family. Their story is yours. Every label that has been given to God's people has been given to you. Through faith in Jesus, this is just a partial list of who you are:

- God's child (Gal. 3:26)
- Part of "a chosen [people], a royal priesthood, a holy nation," and a treasured possession (1 Pet. 2:9)
- A "new creation" (2 Cor. 5:17)
- A member of "the body of Christ" (1 Cor. 12:27)
- God's friend (John 15:15)
- A citizen of heaven (Phil. 3:20)
- An ambassador for Christ (2 Cor. 5:20).

Get Under: Just like an item benefits from being completely under the marinade, we need to get under Scripture. It's been said that we can't understand Scripture until we stand under it. This means that the posture of our hearts can't "stand above" Scripture, picking and choosing what we like and don't like as we read it. Rather, we must "stand under" Scripture and allow the posture of our hearts to be open to God's Word to have authority over us. Much more than just reading Scripture, we must let Scripture read us (see Heb. 4:12).

Take a step back and think about how you approach Scripture. When are you most likely to "stand above" Scripture as described here?

When we stand above Scripture and the posture of our hearts has more authority in our lives than God's Word, it is tempting to believe partial truths or even lies about ourselves rather than the truest things that God says about us.

Get Through: Just like the marinade over time begins to work its way through the item being marinated, we need to let Scripture get through us. Often, people focus on getting through a specific length of Scripture at a time or over the course of a season. For example, while it is wonderful to get through the entire Bible in a year, you may experience a greater impact when you focus more on one passage or biblical truth at a time. Sometimes we need to read and let in the same passage of Scripture for weeks before it really begins to get through and change us.

Let the truth of God's Word get through every layer of who you are. Let it soak into your heart, your mind, and your memories. Re-examine the list of verses on the previous page and pray that God would allow you to trust in this identity for yourself. Take hope in the truth that if you are in Christ, God has given you a new story, a new narrative, that describes you.

Which identifying mark from the list do you find most difficult to believe?

Get Transformed: Just like marinade tenderizes and transforms anything that soaks in it for a long time, God's Word transforms any person who immerses his or her entire life in it. The exponentially beautiful truth of Scripture is that, unlike mere marinade that eventually reaches its limit in transforming an item, there is no limit to the transforming power of God's Word in our lives. We could spend every minute of the rest of our lives soaking in Scripture and we would continue to be transformed through God's Spirit into the image of Jesus more and more.

How have you seen the transforming power of Scripture, either in your life or in the life of someone you know?

THE TRANSFORMING POWER OF SCRIPTURE

As anybody who has ever marinated a piece of chicken, fish, steak, or vegetable knows, it's not enough to just have marinade sitting on the shelf in the same room as the item. The same is true for a Bible that merely sits on a shelf. In fact, it's not enough to simply open up the bottle of marinade. The same is also true for simply opening up the Bible and expecting deep transformation.

Jesus was saturated in the truth of God's Word clearly and continually. He knew who He was and the life God designed and desired for Him to live. He experienced every moment of His life knowing God and being known by Him. As a follower of Jesus, it's essential that we too immerse ourselves in God's Word so that our entire lives can be transformed into the truest lives that God has for us.

Let's take a closer look at a passage we studied in the group time:

> ¹² For the word of God is living and effective and sharper than any double-edged sword, penetrating as far as the separation of soul and spirit, joints and marrow. It is able to judge the thoughts and intentions of the heart. ¹³ No creature is hidden from him, but all things are naked and exposed to the eyes of him to whom we must give an account.
> HEBREWS 4:12-13

Is there an area of your life that currently needs the penetrating and transforming power of God's Word?

What does verse 12 mean when it says God's Word is "living and effective"?

The word *sword* in verse 12 requires some additional attention. This metaphor suggests that the Bible functions much like a surgeon's scalpel when a doctor carefully identifies the location for the incision, penetrates the flesh with the depth that's required, and with great accuracy cuts out the infected area. Similarly, and with the Spirit's guidance, God's Word is a tool that clears away the infected parts of our hearts, transforming us to look more like His Son.

Is this a helpful metaphor? How have you experienced Scripture locating infected areas of your heart?

There are millions of books in print today that are being read throughout the world. Most of us only have the time to read just a few of those each year—and only some of those ever have any kind of meaningful impact on our lives.

The Bible is different. It's on another level than all the other books we can get in our hands. Why? Because it's the very Word of God that tells us about Him and guides us through life. It's living and active. We don't read it so much as we experience its transforming power.

> 105 Your word is a lamp for my feet
> and a light on my path.
> 106 I have solemnly sworn
> to keep your righteous judgments.
> 107 I am severely afflicted;
> LORD, give me life according to your word.
> 108 LORD, please accept my freewill offerings of praise,
> and teach me your judgments.
> 109 My life is constantly in danger,
> yet I do not forget your instruction.
> 110 The wicked have set a trap for me,
> but I have not wandered from your precepts.
> 111 I have your decrees as a heritage forever;
> indeed, they are the joy of my heart.
> 112 I am resolved to obey your statutes
> to the very end.
> PSALM 119:105-112

How does this passage describe a life that's dependent upon God's Word?

How would it change your relationship with God if you allowed Him to narrate your life using the words of Scripture?

SESSION 2

CONNECTED THROUGH PRAYER

Prayer is our response to God's constant

invitation to interact with Him.

REFLECT

We examined in the first session how by immersing ourselves in God's Word we will both discover our identities and build a foundation for transformation to take place in our lives. We learned that the Bible tells us who God is, who we are, and why we exist. And while it's important to read the Bible, *how* we read it may be even more important. Ultimately, being saturated in God's Holy Word will transform how we see God, ourselves, our lives, and the world around us.

In this session, we'll take a look at one of the ways disciples of Jesus should respond to their experiences with God's Word: prayer.

Which of the assignments did you explore this week? How did it go?

What did you learn or experience while reading the Bible?

What questions would you like to ask?

PRAY

Begin the session by connecting with God through prayer. Use the following guidelines as you speak with Him:

- Acknowledge that God alone is worthy of worship, honor, praise, and adoration.

- Thank the all-knowing, all-powerful, perfect God for inviting imperfect people like us to interact with Him.

- Acknowledge that there are so many things pulling our attention away from Him. Ask that God would remove all distractions for this time of study.

- Thank God for being the true source of every good and perfect gift in our lives.

INTRODUCTION

It has been said that there is only one person in the kingdom who can wake up the king at midnight to ask for a glass of water without fear of being punished—the king's kid. Through faith in Jesus, we are the King's kid. Yet we often forget that we have been invited to have limitless interactions with an infinite God. Whether it is because we take it for granted or we allow ourselves to be wrapped up in earthly things, we often neglect and fail to enjoy this tremendous gift of prayer.

As we take a closer look at Jesus' life, it quickly becomes apparent that Jesus consistently responded to God the Father's invitation to interact with Him. Whether Jesus was alone or with others, He was constantly aware of the Father and engaged in continual conversations with Him. Time with God was a critical high priority in Jesus' life.

In the same way that Jesus interacted with God, so too can we. Prayer is far more than a one-way monologue, listing our wishes before God. Instead, prayer can be as dynamic, intimate, and engaging as the way we interact with those closest to us. Prayer involves waiting, listening, remembering, affirming, pleading, petitioning, thanking, confessing, worshiping, and so much more.

To get off on the right foot, we must remember a foundational aspect of prayer: Prayer doesn't actually begin with us; it begins with God. God has already initiated an interaction with us through a variety of ways and means but most fully through His Son, Jesus. Through faith in Christ, we have become the beloved child of the King, who is always welcoming us into His presence. Because prayer is a continuous response to God's interaction, we can have confidence that God hears, knows, and is present to our interactions with Him. Though it may feel like we're the ones initiating the conversation and God is silent, the truth is God is always waiting and inviting us to engage with Him. He is ready, willing, and able to listen, not just to our words but also to our hearts.

Discuss for a moment the ways in which we interact with those closest to us.

Does this description of prayer—our response to God's constant invitation to interact with Him—differ from your perspective of it? If so, how?

KNOW THE STORY

Though you can find numerous examples of Jesus interacting with God throughout the Bible, probably the most famous prayer in all of Scripture is the prayer that Jesus taught His disciples. This is the centerpiece amid the set of foundational teachings on a variety of topics addressed by Christ, commonly referred to as the Sermon on the Mount.

5 "Whenever you pray, you must not be like the hypocrites, because they love to pray standing in the synagogues and on the street corners to be seen by people. Truly I tell you, they have their reward. 6 But when you pray, go into your private room, shut your door, and pray to your Father who is in secret. And your Father who sees in secret will reward you. 7 When you pray, don't babble like the Gentiles, since they imagine they'll be heard for their many words. 8 Don't be like them, because your Father knows the things you need before you ask him.

9 Therefore, you should pray like this:
    Our Father in heaven,
    your name be honored as holy.
    10 Your kingdom come.
    Your will be done
    11 on earth as it is in heaven.
    Give us today our daily bread.
    12 And forgive us our debts,
    as we also have forgiven our debtors.
    13 And do not bring us into temptation,
    but deliver us from the evil one.
MATTHEW 6:5-13

Discuss the differences you see between verses 5-8 and 9-13.

When you read this prayer, what is mentioned that resonates most with what you need from God right now?

UNPACK THE STORY

A MODEL FOR PRAYER

Before teaching the disciples this framework for prayer, Jesus first told them two ways *not* to pray. Jesus first warned them against being like the hypocrites who prayed for show. He then warned them against being like the pagans who babbled empty words. What is wrong with both of these approaches to prayer? Neither was interested in relating and engaging with the one true living God. The first group was uttering words with pomp and circumstance in highly visible public areas like the temple or street corners so that people would see their religious activity and think highly of them. The second group of people from other religions was uttering a high volume of magical, formulaic words, while hoping in vain that their false gods would respond. Jesus reminded His disciples that God sees everything, already knows what they need, and wants to be in close relationship as a father to a child.

How could one's prayer life be transformed if he or she started praying knowing that God sees everything and already knows what we need?

How could one's prayer life be transformed if he or she recognized that the purpose of prayer is to bring us into a closer relationship with God?

Jesus is reminding His listeners and us that prayer isn't the means to get what we want; it's the means to draw near to God and get to know Him better.

The distinguishing characteristic between the groups Jesus warns against and the people Jesus wants us to be is the motivation and means behind why they do what they do. The two groups above pray to use God and people to get closer to things they want. Jesus, however, urges the disciples to be people who pray to get close to the living God.

In this context, Jesus is reminding His listeners and us that prayer isn't the means to get what we want; it's the means to draw near to God and get to know Him better. God is our focus! With that as our primary motivation, the content of the Lord's Prayer then models for us how we can interact with God in a way that draws us closer to Him. Out of the overflow of our response to God's invitation to limitless interaction with Him, we can experience more of the life that God designed and desires for us.

A FRAMEWORK FOR PRAYER

We find six key elements to incorporate into our prayer lives, whether in private or in public, as we delve deeper into the Lord's Prayer as a framework for how we can interact with God.

1. Remembering—"Our Father in heaven"
2. Adoring—"Your name be honored as holy."
3. Inviting—"Your kingdom come ... on earth as it is in heaven."
4. Requesting—"Give us today our daily bread."
5. Confessing/Releasing—"Forgive us our debts, as we also have forgiven our debtors."
6. Petitioning—"Do not bring us into temptation, but deliver us from the evil one."

Using the Lord's Prayer as a framework is a fantastic way to assess your prayer life. Take a few moments to discuss these elements with your group in regard to your own prayer life.

Which of the six elements of the Lord's Prayer do you think will be most natural for you? Which one will be least intuitive for you?

What are ways you can grow in incorporating a specific element into your interactions with God?

Prayer is both the easiest thing and the hardest thing we can do. It is easy in that God constantly invites us to connect with Him through prayer anywhere and anytime. Yet, it is also quite difficult because it requires dependence on God, faith that He loves us, trust that He will show up, and conviction that He will respond and communicate with us. Prayer also requires some hard work on our part—we need to show up regularly and be available, authentic, and vulnerable, so that we can hear whatever God has for us.

Which aspect of prayer have you experienced most recently?

Prayer also requires some hard work on our part—we need to show up regularly and be available, authentic, and vulnerable so that we can hear whatever God has for us.

ENGAGE

Praying together was a frequent practice for the early church. Acts 4:23-31 gives us an example of an actual prayer that Peter and John prayed with other believers. Read and discuss this passage together.

23 After they were released, they went to their own people and reported everything the chief priests and the elders had said to them. 24 When they heard this, they raised their voices together to God and said, "Master, you are the one who made the heaven, the earth, and the sea, and everything in them. 25 You said through the Holy Spirit, by the mouth of our father David your servant:

> Why do the Gentiles rage
> and the peoples plot futile things?
> 26 The kings of the earth take their stand
> and the rulers assemble together
> against the Lord and against his Messiah.

27 "For, in fact, in this city both Herod and Pontius Pilate, with the Gentiles and the people of Israel, assembled together against your holy servant Jesus, whom you anointed, 28 to do whatever your hand and your will had predestined to take place. 29 And now, Lord, consider their threats, and grant that your servants may speak your word with all boldness, 30 while you stretch out your hand for healing, and signs and wonders are performed through the name of your holy servant Jesus." 31 When they had prayed, the place where they were assembled was shaken, and they were all filled with the Holy Spirit and began to speak the word of God boldly.
ACTS 4:23-31

How would you describe the sincerity and passion with which this prayer is voiced?

How is this prayer similar to or different from the typical way you or your group prays?

As you take prayer requests and close in prayer, intentionally incorporate some of the same sincerity and passion from this passage.

In addition to studying God's Word, work with your group leader to create a plan for personal study, worship, and application between now and the next session. Select from the following optional activities to match your personal preferences and available time.

↑ Worship

☑ Read your Bible. Complete the reading plan on page 28.

☐ Spend time with God by engaging the devotional experience on page 29.

☐ Connect with God each day by taking a "prayer walk" around your neighborhood. As you walk past homes and buildings, pray for the people who live or work there. Ask God to move their hearts toward Christ if they do not know Him yet, or if they do, pray for their love for Jesus to be deepened and their lives to reflect Him well.

➡ ⬅ Personal Study

☐ Read and interact with "A Model for Prayer" on page 30.

☐ Read and interact with "A Framework for Prayer" on page 32.

⬅ ➡ Application

☐ Most of Jesus' prayers were not for Himself but for others. This type of intercessory prayer is a wonderful way to care for others and helps us develop more compassionate hearts for them. Pray for someone else in need today, perhaps even for someone who is difficult for you to love. See how God changes your perspective about that person as you pray for him or her over time.

☐ Pray through Psalm 23 this week. Pray through it one line at a time. For example, read verse 1: "The LORD is my shepherd; I have what I need." Then personalize it saying, "Thank You, God, for being the Good Shepherd, the One who loves me and takes good care of me, meeting all of my needs." Continue until you pray through all of the verses.

☐ Memorize Ephesians 6:18: "Pray at all times in the Spirit with every prayer and request, and stay alert with all perseverance and intercession for all the saints."

☐ Other:

WORSHIP

READING PLAN

Read through the following Scripture passages this week. Use the space provided to record your thoughts and responses.

Day 1
Luke 11:1-13

Day 2
Philippians 4:4-7

Day 3
1 Timothy 2:1-7

Day 4
Ephesians 6:10-20

Day 5
James 5:13-18

Day 6
1 Thessalonians 5:16-22

Day 7
Hebrews 4:11-16

MAKE IT PERSONAL

Spend some time during this devotion meditating on and journaling through the Lord's Prayer. Read Matthew 6:9-13 one more time and familiarize yourself with the "A Framework for Prayer" on page 32. Follow its example by personalizing and writing down words that come to mind, Scripture passages that relate, and/or how you've experienced God in relation to each of the elements below:

REMEMBER:

ADORE:

INVITE:

REQUEST:

CONFESS/RELEASE:

PETITION:

A MODEL FOR PRAYER

Throughout the Gospels, Jesus serves as our model for prayer. Scripture shows us who Jesus prayed for, when He prayed, where He prayed, how He prayed, and why He prayed. We would be wise to look to Him as we attempt to strengthen our prayer lives.

So when and where did Jesus pray? The short answer is everywhere and anywhere. In fact, Jesus' prayers never appeared to be repetitive formulas but rather were filled with life, emotion, and rich language that evidenced Jesus' dynamic, deep, constant, and mutually interactive relationship with God the Father. Consider the variety of Jesus' interactions with God that model an anytime-and-everywhere type of prayer life for us.

We have also been invited to experience limitless interaction with God everywhere at anytime. We can interact with God while driving, cleaning, working, playing, laying down, sitting up, running, and so forth. In fact, there is no place or no time in which we cannot interact with God.

Where and when is the most natural place and time for you to interact with God regularly through prayer?

When and where do you have the opportunity to interact with God that you are not currently doing so?

Jesus began His ministry praying (see Luke 4:1-13) and ended His ministry praying from the cross (see Luke 23:34). Jesus prayed in the morning, during the day, and at night. Jesus prayed in the mountains, the wilderness, the garden, and the city. It's no wonder that we've been instructed to pray constantly and everywhere.

Jesus prayed short prayers that spanned just a sentence and long prayers that spanned the entire night. No matter how short or long Jesus interacted with God, He taught us that we should never be repetitious, mistakenly thinking that the more words we use the more God will hear us. Like a relationship with the closest people in our lives, sometimes a few words are all that are needed to communicate the depths of our hearts. Other times, hours in conversation seem to pass by without labor because of the rich, enjoyable connection.

When Jesus prayed, sometimes He made requests of God. He prayed for His needs, His disciples' needs, and our needs. Jesus modeled this for us even though He taught that God already knows our needs before we ask Him. Jesus prayed for those who loved Him and those who rejected Him. Jesus gave thanks to God in His prayers for food, gave thanks for God's nature, and gave thanks that God heard His prayers.

Amid all the requests, prayers for others, and thanksgiving, Jesus trusted God obediently, even in the midst of tremendous anguish. There's no greater evidence of this than Jesus' agony in the garden of Gethsemane where He asked that God would take the cup of suffering away from Him and yet prayed, "nevertheless, not my will, but yours, be done" (Luke 22:42).

Though Jesus taught against praying in public just to be seen by others, Jesus prayed in public for the good of others, showing us that even in public prayer our focus is on God rather than those around us. But even though Jesus prayed in public, we also notice a recurring phrase, "Jesus withdrew." While it would be an accurate observation that Jesus prayed in both public and private, there seems to be a significance to His private prayers—prayers that none of the Gospel writers were able to record because Jesus prayed them after coming apart from the crowd and those closest to Himself.

How does the variety and scope of Jesus' interactions with God through prayer encourage you?

How does Jesus as a model for prayer challenge your current patterns of prayer?

In a world where we can be bombarded with a constant stream of external stimulation, there is a need more than ever to follow Jesus' example of withdrawing into quiet places to cultivate a relationship with God through prayer. The more often we do this, the more quickly we can free ourselves from the burdens and distractions that seek to ensnare us, and the more we will become like Jesus.

A FRAMEWORK FOR PRAYER

Let's be reminded of and dive deeper into the framework of prayer provided for us in the Lord's Prayer. Consider these elements we find in Matthew 6:9-13 as action steps to implement into your prayer life.

> ⁹ "Therefore, you should pray like this:
>   Our Father in heaven,
>   your name be honored as holy.
> ¹⁰ Your kingdom come.
>   Your will be done
> ¹¹ on earth as it is in heaven.
>   Give us today our daily bread.
> ¹² And forgive us our debts,
>   as we also have forgiven our debtors.
> ¹³ And do not bring us into temptation,
>   but deliver us from the evil one.
> MATTHEW 6:9-13

Remembering—"Our Father in heaven": We begin our interaction with God acknowledging who He has revealed Himself to be. He is our Father, Creator, Sustainer, Provider, Protector, and so much more. He is all-powerful, all-knowing, and all-sufficient. As we immerse our lives in God's Word, we can learn more about who God has revealed Himself to be.

Adoring—"Your name be honored as holy": We continue our interaction with God acknowledging that His character and His reputation are worthy of our fully-surrendered worship. We remember God's faithfulness throughout Scripture and in our lives. We acknowledge and affirm that God is who God says He is, and we respond in worship. We value God's truth and His direction over the opinion of others.

Inviting—"Your kingdom come ... on earth as it is in heaven": We invite God's reign and rule which is perfect in heaven to be present in our lives and in our world. We submit to God's ways as being superior to our ways.

Requesting—"Give us today our daily bread": We ask for today's needs. We don't worry about tomorrow or get ahead of ourselves planning. We share the concerns we have for ourselves and others even as we acknowledge God's sovereignty and power to change people and situations according to His perfect will. We freely ask for what we want, while trusting that God in His grace and love will provide what is best for us.

Confessing/Releasing—"Forgive us our debts, as we also have forgiven our debtors": We embrace our forgiveness through Jesus' power over sin in our lives even as we extend forgiveness through Jesus' power over those who have hurt us. We release our feelings of shame to God, our pain from others, and our need to condemn others.

Petitioning—"Do not bring us into temptation, but deliver us from the evil one": We ask for God's leading moving forward, a renewed focus on His design and desire for us, and protection from anything that distracts us from life with Him.

Learn from this framework of prayer and incorporate it into your prayer life. Be intentional about interacting with God in each of the areas of remembering, adoring, inviting, requesting, confessing, releasing, and petitioning.

Which one of these elements do you have the most difficulty with? Why do you think it is so difficult?

Scripture refers to Jesus withdrawing Himself from potential distractions to pray. Identify a place and a time of day that you can withdraw to spend uninterrupted and focused time in order to interact with God.

SESSION 3
LIVING IN COMMUNITY

We are called to live authentically
and interdependently with one
another in biblical community.

REFLECT

As we learned in the previous session, prayer is an invitation to interact with our Creator. Prayer isn't a presentation of our wish list to God. It involves waiting, listening, remembering, affirming, pleading, petitioning, thanking, confessing, worshiping, and so much more. God is ready, willing, and able to listen not just to our words but also our hearts. Because of Christ, we have become children of the Father, who is always welcoming us into His presence.

Which of the assignments did you explore this week? How did it go?

What did you learn or experience while reading the Bible?

What questions would you like to ask?

PRAY

Begin the session by connecting with God through prayer. Use the following guidelines as you speak with Him:

- Ask God to show us how we have been created for community and the ways in which we can cultivate community as disciples of Jesus.

- Thank God for your church family with whom you worship, pray, and serve, for how He has used other believers to help you grow, and for the group of people you are with at this moment.

- Acknowledge and praise God that the brothers and sisters who share your faith and commitment to following Jesus are a gift from God to encourage you in the ups and downs of life.

- Ask the Holy Spirit to intervene in this time of study that you may build more authentic relationships that move you forward in loving God and loving others.

INTRODUCTION

Beyond the city limits of San Francisco exists a land of giants—redwood trees so tall that if they were to lay down on a football-field-length bed their feet would hang off the edge another 10 feet. Their trunks are so wide that a school bus could hide behind and you'd never see it. In the Armstrong Redwoods National State Reserve, there is even a tree that is estimated to have stood tall for more than 1,400 years.

While so many are amazed by these ancient trees as they extend skyward toward the heavens, what is even more awe-inspiring is how they have extended underground. It is the root system of these ancient redwood trees that has enabled them to stand strong against threatening winds and violent storms that could rip them from their foundation. Yet, their roots do not extend vertically deep into the ground. Surprisingly, redwood tree roots typically go no more than 12 feet below ground, hardly enough to sustain 300-feet-tall trees through the centuries of destructive weather. So, how is it possible that redwoods have survived in this area, enabling countless people to stand in wonder with eyes toward the heavens to take in the sights of the tallest living things on this planet? The answer can be summed up in one word—*community*.

Amazingly, these ancient redwoods have underground roots that extend outwards of 150 feet, interlocking with the root systems of other redwoods in the grove. Beneath the feet of visiting onlookers, these giants hold one another up in a community of interwoven roots. Because of this, their stability and strength is multiplied as their foundation becomes larger than their height. They have been able to grow large and strong because they have done it together.

What are some words or emotions that come to mind when you picture an ancient redwood grove with a vast root system that is interwoven and interdependent upon each other?

How does the metaphor of the redwoods describe the church?

The only way we can endure the storms of life and thrive as God intended us to is through our fellow believers. Our spiritual roots must extend, not just deep but wide, spread among the lives of those around us. Just as there is no redwood tree that has endured for centuries without the help of other redwood trees, there is no such thing as a disciple who thrives without the community of other disciples.

KNOW THE STORY

The first followers of Jesus were some of the most diverse people you could imagine. There were zealots (like Simon) who came from a radicalized political party that were known for assassinating government officials (like Matthew, a tax collector). There were former pagans who enjoyed eating food that any Jewish person would not only find repulsive but against Mosaic Law. There were misfits, social pariahs, men, women, children, singles, marrieds, widows, orphans, type A's, cynics, and those with low self-esteem. Yet, this diverse community was remarkably unified around one thing: Jesus.

The Book of Acts chronicles the 30 years of the early church's explosion beyond social, geographic, ethnic, and religious boundaries through the power of the Holy Spirit. The author, Luke, records with much detail, giving us many moving pictures of the type of community that can be cultivated amid tremendous diversity and adversity. They were often violently persecuted and yet they were as committed to one another as they were committed to their Savior. Rather than using the community to build up their individual resources and agendas, individuals in the early church used their resources to build up the community of believers.

What are some things we do in life that are easier to accomplish with a community of people?

Briefly discuss the similarities and differences between your relationships with other believers and with non-believers.

One of the foundational descriptions of the early church is found in Acts 2, where Luke writes,

> [42] They devoted themselves to the apostles' teaching, to the fellowship, to the breaking of bread, and to prayer. [43] Everyone was filled with awe, and many wonders and signs were being performed through the apostles. [44] Now all the believers were together and held all things in common. [45] They sold their possessions and property and distributed the proceeds to all, as any had need. [46] Every day they devoted themselves to meeting together in the temple, and broke bread from house to house. They ate their food with joyful and sincere hearts, [47] praising God and enjoying the favor of all the people. Every day the Lord added to their number those who were being saved.
> ACTS 2:42-47

UNPACK THE STORY
EXPERIENCING LIFE TOGETHER

The richness of the Greek language must also be noted to grasp the depth of community this diverse group of people experienced. In Acts 2, we find the word "together" mentioned twice in our English translation. However, two different Greek words are used in each of these instances and once understood, you'll never think of "together" the same way again.

The first Greek word is *epi*. It's a word that is used to describe the physical location of something. Luke basically is telling us that the first followers of Jesus were in close proximity to one another. They didn't see each other twice a month; rather the first followers of Jesus frequently rubbed shoulders with one another, ate, prayed, worshiped, and experienced the richness of life together.

However, just having proximity with one another doesn't lead to deep, authentic, biblical community. Perhaps this is why Luke uses a different Greek word later in Acts 2 to describe this group of people living in proximity with one another. The second Greek word is *homothumadon,* and it's a word on an entirely different level than *epi*. Its meaning transcends physical space and is a togetherness that occurs on a deeper spiritual and emotional level. It's only found 12 times in the New Testament, and Luke uses the word 11 times in Acts.

> The first followers of Jesus frequently rubbed shoulders with one another, ate, prayed, worshiped, and experienced the richness of life together.

What about this Acts 2 description of biblical community is appealing? What about it is terrifying?

Why do you think many people find it difficult to be meaningfully devoted to a group of believers?

Knit together by the Holy Spirit dwelling within them and hearts ablaze and fixed on Jesus, their world (and the world) was turned upside down because of the depth of their community.

COMMUNITY VS. PROXIMITY

On our discipleship journey, it's common to mistake proximity for community. It's easy to think that "being around" other followers of Jesus is what it means to be in community. However, proximity and community are two distinctive things that result in two different outcomes.

In the same way that redwood tree root systems offer us an apt metaphor for community, tree nurseries offer us a vivid picture of proximity. Tree nurseries, like the natural environment for redwoods, are filled with many trees. In tree nurseries, the trees are growing and are healthy. From a distance, the trees in a tree nursery appear to be in community with one another. They are closely situated, and in some cases, their branches are even touching one another.

However, when a strong storm rips through a tree nursery, many trees are toppled over, unable to stand like the redwoods. The difference is that the trees in a nursery have never truly been in community, they have only been in proximity. Each tree in a nursery exists within its own planter box. The trees in tree nurseries grow, but only in isolation. Their roots extend, yet they are never able to get the stability that redwoods have because they are not interconnected or interdependent. True, some of the trees in the nursery don't topple over, giving the illusion of stability. However, it's likely that the trees still standing are located on the interior of the nursery while the trees on the fringes of the nursery have taken the fall.

Why is proximity necessary, but a shallow substitute for community?

Why do our groups and our churches so often settle for mere proximity rather than pursue true biblical community?

If you cultivate community, you always get proximity.

Much of what we call community in our church today is simply proximity. Standing next to one another in a worship service, serving alongside one another on a project, even sitting on a couch with the same people week after week doesn't necessarily mean that community is being cultivated. If you settle for proximity, you rarely get deep community. However, if you cultivate community, you always get proximity.

ENGAGE

Scripture is flooded with what has been referred to as "one another" verses—100 times in the New Testament to be exact. These verses help us go beyond proximity and begin to cultivate deep, authentic, biblical community. These verses are not just suggestions or recommendations from Scripture, but in many cases, they are framed in the imperative, as commands to be obeyed.

Several of these "one another" verses call us to encourage one another. This is a key aspect of life together in biblical community. To practice this in a concrete way, prepare index cards that have the name of each person in the group on individual cards. Ask everyone to write an encouraging note for each person in the group. This could be something they appreciate about the person or how they have seen God work in that person. If they don't know the person it could be framed as a prayer that God would use this person in a significant way. Once you have finished with one card, pass the card to the right and continue with the next card. Eventually the card will return to the person whose name is on it. This is a powerful way to affirm each person and the ways in which God is working in them.

What are your observations from this activity?

What are some things that would happen to a biblical community if encouragement and affirmation were common practice?

PRAYER REQUESTS

In addition to studying God's Word, work with your group leader to create a plan for personal study, worship, and application between now and the next session. Select from the following optional activities to match your personal preferences and available time.

⬆ Worship

☑ Read your Bible. Complete the reading plan on page 42.

☐ Spend time with God by engaging the devotional experience on page 43.

☐ Connect with God each day through prayer. Pick one or two characteristics of the Acts 2 church that you aren't currently experiencing. Pray that God would reveal action plans for you to incorporate into your community. Take time to listen to all God has to say.

➡ ⬅ Personal Study

☐ Read and interact with "Experiencing Life Together" on page 44.

☐ Read and interact with "One Anothers" on page 46.

⬅ ➡ Application

☐ God often uses people to change people. Journal about a time when God used another person or a group of believers to encourage or challenge you to move toward Jesus and His way of life. Likewise, share a time when you were used by God to encourage or challenge someone else.

☐ Connect with someone from your group this week. Make an appointment to meet for coffee or lunch. When you meet, ask each other two questions: (1) How has God been working in you and your life lately? and (2) How can I pray for you? Then plan to follow up in the coming weeks.

☐ Memorize John 13:34-35: "I give you a new command: Love one another. Just as I have loved you, you are also to love one another. By this everyone will know that you are my disciples, if you love one another."

☐ Other:

 **WORSHIP**

READING PLAN

Read through the following Scripture passages this week. Use the space provided to record your thoughts and responses.

Day 1
Romans 12:3-13

Day 2
Philippians 2:1-13

Day 3
Hebrews 10:19-25

Day 4
Ecclesiastes 4:1-16

Day 5
1 Peter 4:7-11

Day 6
1 Corinthians 12:12-31

Day 7
John 15:12-17

TOGETHER

The believers we see in Acts 2 weren't just an affinity group that got together on a semi-regular basis and enjoyed an activity together. They experienced life together. There were no isolated "lone ranger Christians." Far from it. They immersed their lives in God's Word together, prayed together, shared each other's burdens, laughed together, cried together, parented together, ate together, celebrated the Lord's Supper together, lived with thanksgiving together, served together, gave sacrificially together, and were daily hospitable to newcomers together.

Every member of this Acts 2 group knew each other and they were known by one another. They belonged. They were embraced. They were challenged. They experienced conflict and reconciliation. They forgave and were forgiven. They loved and were loved. This small, ever-growing group was able to change the world because they focused on God's mission together.

Make two lists of deeds and activities the early Christians did together that you are currently experiencing with other believers and that you would like to experience with other believers.

Already Doing   *Not Yet Doing*

What are some of the barriers to true fellowship or authentic "life-on-life" relationships in our culture today? What are some cultural values we hold that hinder our interdependence upon one another?

EXPERIENCING LIFE TOGETHER

Let's look closer at the second meaning for the English word "together" we find in Acts 2: *Homothumadon*. Perhaps you have experienced glimpses of *homothumadon*. If you've ever been part of a large crowd at a concert and everyone in attendance is singing along to that song everyone has been waiting for, that is *homothumadon*. Or if you've been to a sporting event and tens of thousands of fans erupt into celebration when their team scores the game winner—that's a taste of *homothumadon* as we see it in Acts 2. It's literally a mob mentality where the many become one, caught up in something greater and bigger than themselves.

Homothumadon is a combination of words that literally mean "the same fiery passion." Some English versions use the tame translation, "one accord," but *homothumadon* has the intensity of a unified crowd. And when used to describe the early church, it was the most beautiful riot ever witnessed. It was a riot of belonging, service, love, patience, hospitality, inclusiveness, and so much more. Yes, the early church was in physical proximity together, but they were also dynamically and spiritually together.

> *Take some time to describe your best experience with a small community of believers. What are the elements that made that community supportive and memorable?*

> *How did God use the people in that community to impact your life?*

As this *epi-* and *homothumadon*-rich community swelled in size, even passionate enemies of the early church were transformed and brought into the very community they once hated. Though there were many examples throughout history, perhaps one of the most famous is found in Scripture—the self-righteous Saul who became the Christ-focused Paul after encountering the resurrected Jesus on a road. As Paul began experiencing the transforming effects of a Christ-centered community, and as he grew in his faith, he became one of the greatest champions of biblical community.

In one of his letters to the community of Christians in Corinth, Paul borrowed the metaphor of the human body to instruct his readers on how much they need one another in community.

¹² For just as the body is one and has many parts, and all the parts of that body, though many, are one body—so also is Christ. ¹³ For we were all baptized by one Spirit into one body—whether Jews or Greeks, whether slaves or free—and we were all given one Spirit to drink. ¹⁴ Indeed, the body is not one part but many. ¹⁵ If the foot should say, "Because I'm not a hand, I don't belong to the body," it is not for that reason any less a part of the body. ¹⁶ And if the ear should say, "Because I'm not an eye, I don't belong to the body," it is not for that reason any less a part of the body. ¹⁷ If the whole body were an eye, where would the hearing be? If the whole body were an ear, where would the sense of smell be? ¹⁸ But as it is, God has arranged each one of the parts in the body just as he wanted. ¹⁹ And if they were all the same part, where would the body be? ²⁰ As it is, there are many parts, but one body.

1 CORINTHIANS 12:12-20

Paul then goes on to say that some members of the body can't say, "I don't need you," because that would make as much sense as a parched mouth saying to a pair of hands, "I don't need you to pick up that glass of water for me." The parts not only need to work together but are essential to each other. The word Paul uses is rare in our world: *indispensable*. Paul speaks this surprising word in describing each member of the community of believers and even declares, "The parts of the body that seem to be weaker are indispensable" (1 Cor. 12:22b, ESV).

Some may often feel superior to others and attempt to live life on their own. Others may feel like the weak link, always bringing others down. But Paul insists that all parts of the body, every member in a biblical community, has value and should be considered indispensable. List below specific examples of how you have seen this to be true in your community.

This is a truth that must be grasped to experience the type of community that God designs and desires for those who are His. We must choose to step into our indispensability and recognize and celebrate the indispensability of others. Not only do we need each other in indispensable ways but we are indispensably needed by others—amid all of our flaws, insecurities, strengths, weaknesses, and spiritual gifts.

ONE ANOTHERS

In the group time, we briefly talked about the large number of "one another" verses in Scripture—100 times in the New Testament. Below are just 40 of these verses we find from God's Word. Resist the temptation to skip ahead to the questions. We cannot grow as disciples apart from practicing these mandates with each other in the body of Christ.

1. "Be at peace with one another" (Mark 9:50).
2. "Wash one another's feet" (John 13:14).
3. "Love one another" (John 13:34; 15:12,17).
4. "Love one another deeply as brothers and sisters" (Rom. 12:10).
5. "Outdo one another in showing honor" (Rom. 12:10).
6. "Live in harmony with one another" (Rom. 12:16).
7. "Love one another" (Rom. 13:8).
8. "Let us no longer judge one another" (Rom. 14:13).
9. "Accept one another, just as Christ also accepted you" (Rom. 15:7).
10. "Instruct one another" (Rom. 15:14).
11. "When you come together to eat, welcome one another" (1 Cor. 11:33).
12. "Have the same concern for each other" (1 Cor. 12:25).
13. "Serve one another through love" (Gal. 5:13).
14. "Let us not become conceited, provoking one another, envying one another" (Gal. 5:26).
15. "Carry one another's burdens" (Gal. 6:2).
16. "With patience, bearing with one another in love" (Eph. 4:2).
17. "Be kind and compassionate to one another" (Eph. 4:32).
18. "Forgiving one another" (Eph. 4:32).
19. Speak "to one another in psalms, hymns and spiritual songs" (Eph. 5:19).
20. Submit "to one another in the fear of Christ" (Eph. 5:21).
21. "In humility consider others as more important than yourselves" (Phil. 2:3).
22. "Do not lie to one another" (Col. 3:9).
23. Forgive "one another if anyone has a grievance against another" (Col. 3:13).
24. Teach one another "in all wisdom" (Col. 3:16).
25. Admonish "one another" (Col. 3:16).
26. "May the Lord cause you to increase and overflow with love for one another" (1 Thess. 3:12).
27. "Encourage one another" (1 Thess. 4:18).
28. "Build each other up" (1 Thess. 5:11).
29. "Encourage each other daily" (Heb. 3:13).
30. "Let us watch out for one another to provoke love and good works" (Heb. 10:24).
31. "Don't criticize one another" (Jas. 4:11).

32. "Do not complain about one another" (Jas. 5:9).

33. "Confess your sins to one another" (Jas. 5:16).

34. "Pray for one another" (Jas. 5:16).

35. "All of you be like-minded and sympathetic" (1 Pet. 3:8).

36. "Love one another, and be compassionate and humble" (1 Pet. 3:8).

37. "Maintain constant love for one another" (1 Pet. 4:8).

38. "Be hospitable to one another without complaining" (1 Pet. 4:9).

39. "Just as each one has received a gift, use it to serve others" (1 Pet. 4:10).

40. "Clothe yourselves with humility toward one another" (1 Pet. 5:5).

Which of these "one anothers" comes naturally to you?

Which of these "one anothers" is tough to apply and why?

What specifically can you learn from and begin to implement into your life in regard to the emphasis Scripture places on community?

John 13:35 says the world will know we are Christians by our love for each other. If a nonbeliever were to observe the relationships within your small group, your ministry team or your church, what would they conclude about Jesus? Are these relationships with other believers marked by the characteristics of Christ or the fruit of His Spirit? When it comes to the communities you are attached to, these are important questions to think about and pray through. We need to constantly have these "one another" verses on our hearts, asking God which verses we need to live out more and in what relationship we need to apply them.

SPIRIT-FILLED LIFE

The Holy Spirit indwells, empowers, and transforms us to live in tune with God.

REFLECT

In the previous session we learned that disciples of Jesus are called to live authentically and interdependently with one another in biblical community. Living in proximity with each other isn't enough. Like the root system of the redwood trees, our lives must be interconnected to experience deep, biblical community.

In this session, we'll examine the role of the Holy Spirit in that community, as well as in our lives as individuals.

Which of the assignments did you explore this week? How did it go?

What did you learn or experience while reading the Bible?

What questions would you like to ask?

PRAY

Begin the session by connecting with God through prayer. Use the following guidelines as you speak with Him:

- Thank God for the Holy Spirit who helps us pray and also intercedes for us when we don't know how to pray for ourselves or for each other.

- Invite the Holy Spirit to guide, teach, and empower your group during discussion.

- Pray that through the power of the Holy Spirit, God will empower us to become more like Jesus.

INTRODUCTION

If you've ever replaced the strings on a guitar you'll notice something. Brand new strings have a tough time staying on pitch. It usually takes a while for the strings to adjust to the correct tension and requires frequent tightening to match the pitch of a tuner. The new strings need to be played often until they can acclimate closer to the correct pitch. After a couple months of regular playing only minor tweaks are needed each day to get the strings in tune. Listening to the tuner and adjusting the strings is always the first step before playing a single note. This must not be skipped if we want to make beautiful music.

In a similar way, before we put our faith in Christ, we were like a hopelessly out-of-tune instrument, incapable of being in sync with the God of the universe. As the Bible points out in Romans 3:23, "all have sinned and fall short of the glory of God." Sin had separated us from God until Jesus Christ saved us through His death, burial, and resurrection. As soon as we receive this gift of grace, we are filled with the Holy Spirit who, like the perfect tuning fork, reveals areas of our lives that need to change and empowers us to be more in tune with God. Over time, as we experience more of God and become increasingly more like Jesus we may need smaller adjustments. However, we will always need to be constantly aligning ourselves with the Spirit's perfect pitch.

Think about an experience when you heard (or sang) something out of tune. What words would you use to describe the effect of such music on you or other listeners?

Share a time, moment, day, or season of life when you sensed you were living in tune with God. Describe the circumstances surrounding this experience.

Throughout Scripture, and most fully in the life of Jesus Christ, we get an accurate picture of what it means to live a life perfectly in tune with God. Yet, we're completely unable to do this on our own. Thankfully, God sent us Jesus to be a model for us and then sent believers the gift of the Holy Spirit to help us become the people He created us to be. It's God's own Spirit that works in and through us to make us more like Jesus. As disciples of Jesus, we can joyfully embrace the reality that God's Spirit dwells within us, empowers us, and transforms us to live in tune with God's desires and plans for us.

KNOW THE STORY

Last week we visited the end of Acts 2 to discover how the early church interacted together in a biblical community. Let's now rewind in the chapter to see what it was that brought this community together.

¹ When the day of Pentecost had arrived, they were all together in one place. ² Suddenly a sound like that of a violent rushing wind came from heaven, and it filled the whole house where they were staying. ³ They saw tongues like flames of fire that separated and rested on each one of them. ⁴ Then they were all filled with the Holy Spirit and began to speak in different tongues, as the Spirit enabled them. ⁵ Now there were Jews staying in Jerusalem, devout people from every nation under heaven. ⁶ When this sound occurred, a crowd came together and was confused because each one heard them speaking in his own language. ⁷ They were astounded and amazed, saying, "Look, aren't all these who are speaking Galileans? ⁸ How is it that each of us can hear them in our own native language? ⁹ Parthians, Medes, Elamites; those who live in Mesopotamia, in Judea and Cappadocia, Pontus and Asia, ¹⁰ Phrygia and Pamphylia, Egypt and the parts of Libya near Cyrene; visitors from Rome (both Jews and converts), ¹¹ Cretans and Arabs—we hear them declaring the magnificent acts of God in our own tongues." ¹² They were all astounded and perplexed, saying to one another, "What does this mean? "
ACTS 2:1-12

What do you find interesting about this account? Why?

What did you observe about the Holy Spirit from this passage?

In this tremendous and awe-inspiring moment in the life of God's people, the "power" that Jesus promised in Acts 1:8 was given to all the believers so that they could be witnesses to the life and love of Jesus "in Jerusalem ... and to the end of the earth" (Acts 1:8).

UNPACK THE STORY
THE HOLY SPIRIT IN SCRIPTURE

Occurring on the Festival of Pentecost, which was 50 days after Passover, there were religious pilgrims from all over the world who had traveled to Jerusalem to celebrate the event. In Acts 2, the believers spoke in "tongues," or languages, not otherworldly or unintelligible languages. Rather, as Luke recounts the event, people from all nations were able to hear in their own native language all the wonderful things that God had done.

This is a complete reversal of a similar scene in Genesis 11 surrounding the Tower of Babel. At the Tower of Babel, people were fragmented after God confused the language of all the earth as a result of their pride in attempting to build a tower to the heavens to make a name for themselves. Here at Pentecost, people were unified after God made known the gospel in the languages of the people present, which resulted in the believers boasting in the name of Jesus.

Responding to the question asked in Acts 2:12, Peter addressed the swelling crowd. Through the Holy Spirit, people were able to hear the gospel being presented in their own language. As a result, 3,000 people became believers and made the decision to be baptized. In the same way the Gospel of Luke begins with the birth of our Savior, the Acts of the Apostles begins with the birth of the church, setting the stage for the outward ministry explosion ahead. Through the power of the Holy Spirit, the first disciples of Jesus were sent out amid persecution, proclaiming the gospel of Jesus to the ends of the earth.

> Through the power of the Holy Spirit, the first disciples of Jesus were sent out amid persecution, proclaiming the gospel of Jesus to the ends of the earth.

If you had been there that day, how do you think you would have responded? Why?

Though the Holy Spirit makes His entrance at the beginning of Acts 2, the Holy Spirit was at work long before that moment at Pentecost. In fact, Scripture describes the relational nature of God as God the Father, God the Spirit, and God the Son. Existing eternally as a distinct member of the Triune Godhead, God's Spirit was present at creation, is the source of life, is our Teacher and Guide, and is the manifestation of God's presence. God's Spirit filled and equipped people in the Old Testament and empowered Jesus' ministry, enabling Him to atone for the sins of the world, judge the world, overthrow the wicked, and reign in justice and righteousness.

THE WORK OF THE HOLY SPIRIT

Jesus spoke often about the Holy Spirit, instructing His disciples to wait for the Holy Spirit since the Spirit was the promise of the Father (see Luke 24:49). Related to this, Jesus on numerous occasions emphasized that it would be God the Father who would send the Spirit to the disciples to teach and remind them of everything that Jesus had already taught.

What is so significant about the events at Pentecost is that every believer since that moment has received the gift of God's Spirit. In the Old Testament, God's Spirit would come and go, but ever since Pentecost, God's Spirit permanently dwells in each believer, signifying that we belong to God.

> *What does it mean that God's Spirit permanently dwells in us, signifying that we belong to God?*

The work of God's Spirit has existed eternally and throughout human history in many active ways, but we also see from Scripture that the Spirit is active in our lives today in a number of ways. Like the early church, each believer receives the Holy Spirit the moment he or she becomes a believer. God's Spirit knows us in our weaknesses, intercedes for us in prayer, helps us understand Scripture, engages us in corporate worship, comforts us during crisis situations, reveals Jesus' purpose for us, reminds us of our identity in Christ, convicts us of our sin, and supports us as we share the gospel with others.

The Holy Spirit also gives individual members of the body of Christ spiritual gifts to build up and empower the church. In the New Testament, we get a picture of the work of the Holy Spirit that individually gifts us but collectively unifies and builds us up to function as the church (see 1 Cor. 12; Eph. 4). Love and unity are given as credible evidence that the Holy Spirit is operating through a group of people, enabling Christ to be revealed in and through us.

God's Spirit knows us in our weaknesses, intercedes for us in prayer, helps us understand Scripture, and supports us as we share the gospel with others.

> *Review all the ways we can experience the Holy Spirit listed above. Discuss how you have personally experienced the Holy Spirit in some of these examples.*

ENGAGE

As a group, identify songs that embody the definition of "great music." After identifying this, take in all of its parts that come together in harmonious ways to create attractive music. Notice how each instrument is in tune with one another, each voice meshes well with the others, and each chord and progression lead to a beautiful unified whole.

After spending some time discussing the qualities of the music you identified, discuss the concept of living "in tune" with God.

What are descriptions of an individual who is "in tune" with God's Spirit?

What are some specific actions a community of believers can carry out that indicate they are collectively "in tune" with the Holy Spirit?

PRAYER REQUESTS

....
....
....
....
....
....
....
....
....
....
....
....

In addition to studying God's Word, work with your group leader to create a plan for personal study, worship, and application between now and the next session. Select from the following optional activities to match your personal preferences and available time.

⬆ Worship

☑ Read your Bible. Complete the reading plan on page 56.

☐ Spend time with God by engaging the devotional experience on page 57.

☐ Connect with God each day by specifically praying to the Holy Spirit—asking Him to intercede for you, to help you understand Scripture through your reading this week, to reveal Jesus' purposes for you, and to remind you of your identity in Jesus.

➡ ⬅ Personal Study

☐ Read and interact with "A Study of the Holy Spirit from Paul's Perspective" on page 58.

☐ Read and interact with "The Holy Spirit's Nine-Note Scale" on page 60.

⬅ ➡ Application

☐ Read Galatians 5:22-23 and identify one person for each of the nine characteristics of the fruit of the Spirit. The goal is to grow in all of these characteristics, but for this activity, think of one person for each of the characteristics listed. Contact each person this week and affirm how you have seen this characteristic displayed in his or her life.

☐ Memorize 2 Corinthians 3:18: "We all, with unveiled faces, are looking as in a mirror at the glory of the Lord and are being transformed into the same image from glory to glory; this is from the Lord who is the Spirit."

☐ Journal your experiences. Be aware and take note of all the times you have seen the work of the Spirit this week. This could be from an experience you had sharing the gospel with someone. It could be during your time alone with God in prayer and Scripture reading. You may also take note of how you experienced the Spirit during a time of corporate worship.

☐ Other:

 **WORSHIP**

READING PLAN

Read through the following Scripture passages this week. Use the space provided to record your thoughts and responses.

Day 1
John 14:25-26

Day 2
Ephesians 5:18-20

Day 3
2 Corinthians 3:7-18

Day 4
Romans 8:18-27

Day 5
Ezekiel 36:22-38

Day 6
John 16:5-15

Day 7
Galatians 5:16-26

IN TUNE

An essential element of music isn't only notes that are in tune but also rhythm that is consistent. By definition, sound without rhythm is noise. Sadly, many of our lives are lived at such a frantic and hurried pace that the sound of our lives is more akin to noise rather than music. The God who is revealed in Scripture is a God of rhythm. We see this clearly in the Genesis 1 creation account where the description of all things being created happens in six days followed by a day of rest. Much more beautiful than just noise, God created everything and according to Zephaniah 3:17, He rejoices over His people with singing.

We were created for a rhythm that lines up with God's rhythm. It's from a place of rest that the music of our lives comes forth. Look at some of the following passages that address seeking out a place of rest and peace in your life by staying in tune with the Spirit and in rhythm with God the Father.

> [12] Moses said to the LORD, "Look, you have told me, 'Lead this people up,' but you have not let me know whom you will send with me. You said, 'I know you by name, and you have also found favor with me.' [13] Now if I have indeed found favor with you, please teach me your ways, and I will know you, so that I may find favor with you. Now consider that this nation is your people." [14] And he replied, "My presence will go with you, and I will give you rest."
> EXODUS 33:12-14

> [28] "Come to me, all of you who are weary and burdened, and I will give you rest. [29] Take up my yoke and learn from me, because I am lowly and humble in heart, and you will find rest for your souls. [30] For my yoke is easy and my burden is light."
> MATTHEW 11:28-30

> Now may the God of hope fill you with all joy and peace as you believe so that you may overflow with hope by the power of the Holy Spirit.
> ROMANS 15:13

In the same way, choose to begin adjusting the rhythm of your life in small, tangible ways. Perhaps you might start each day from the restful place of prayer or Scripture reading before you begin to read your emails or pick up your phone. It may be a daily or weekly conversation you initiate between a friend or a family member, talking through how you've experienced God lately. Whatever small step you choose, pray that God's Spirit will guide it to a healthy and soul-enriching rhythm in your life.

A STUDY OF THE HOLY SPIRIT FROM PAUL'S PERSPECTIVE

Paul made attempts to live in tune with God's design and desire. In Philippians 3:4-6, he even says that according to the law he was "blameless." However, Paul's conclusion was that all these things added up to "dung" (v. 8). In other words, he was living out of tune. However, he didn't realize he was living out of tune until he encountered Jesus in all of His perfection. As a result, Paul was willing to trade his "out of tune" life for knowing Jesus "and the power of his resurrection" (v. 10). Then, the rest of Paul's life was an ongoing journey of tuning and re-tuning his life through the power of the Holy Spirit. Like Paul, we can choose to live either in tune or out of tune, in harmony or in cacophony.

> *In the same way Paul came to the conclusion he was living a life out of tune with God, describe a time when you realized you were living out of tune.*

> *What spiritual disciplines, relationships, or experiences have helped you get back in alignment or help keep you in alignment with God?*

As Paul was on a journey of living in tune with God through the power of the Holy Spirit, he taught and equipped others to do the same. In his missionary journeys and letters to the churches, we see some of his teaching that reminds us of the Holy Spirit's integral role in living in tune as individuals and as a community of disciples.

In 2 Corinthians 3:18 he writes that "We all, with unveiled faces, are looking as in a mirror at the glory of the Lord and are being transformed into the same image from glory to glory; this is from the Lord who is the Spirit." In other words, through the Holy Spirit we are continually being fine tuned to become more like Jesus. Though we can't live in tune on our own power, through God's Spirit, our lives will begin to resonate more and more with Jesus who lived a life perfectly in tune. God never gives up on us and His Spirit is constantly at work empowering and guiding us.

What words or emotions come to mind when you learn that God is continually tuning your life to become more like Jesus?

As we well know, there are things in our lives that can quickly cause us to get out of tune. In Galatians 5:17 Paul writes, "For the flesh desires what is against the Spirit, and the Spirit desires what is against the flesh; these are opposed to each other, so that you don't do what you want."

Paul goes on to list two different ways of living: works of the flesh and fruit of the Spirit. To paraphrase, these two different ways of living are not compatible and can never be in harmony with one another. A life filled with works of the flesh—such as envy, anger, and jealousy—will always clash with a life filled with fruit of the Spirit—such as joy, love, and self-control.

Though we might choose to live by the Spirit, works of the flesh will continue to be a temptation in our lives. There will most likely be moments or even seasons where we stop listening or obeying God and get out of tune. It's essential that we don't give up on the journey that God is committed to in our lives.

In Philippians 1:6, Paul writes: "I am sure of this, that he who started a good work in you will carry it on to completion until the day of Christ Jesus." In other words, God always finishes what He starts. No matter how difficult or out of tune you may feel as a disciple of Jesus, God will complete that work in and through you until the day you are face to face with Christ.

Tuning an instrument is critical to making music, especially in combination with other instruments. As you think through this week of study thus far, how does the Holy Spirit help us be in tune with God's purposes and desires for us?

PERSONAL STUDY 2

THE HOLY SPIRIT'S NINE-NOTE SCALE

The apostle Paul's metaphor of "the fruit of the Spirit" could be paraphrased to "notes of the Spirit" as a way to describe the sound of a life that is "in tune" with God. Living a life that is in tune with the Holy Spirit is to resonate the nine-note scale of love, joy, peace, patience, kindness, goodness, faithfulness, gentleness, and self-control as described in Galatians 5:22-23. To tune our lives to anything other than the Spirit is to live "off key." Our lives, like instruments, desperately need the true pitch of the Holy Spirit as our tuning fork.

An easy test to see if we are out of tune is to reflect on the words, thoughts, and actions in our lives, while at the same time considering the nine-note scale from the Spirit. If our lives are out of tune, then there is something other than the Holy Spirit resonating within us. Sometimes it is fear, anxiety, pride, lack of trust, or an inability to remember who God is and who God created us to be that causes us to get out of tune. As a follower of Jesus, we have God's Spirit dwelling inside of us and we can make the choice to cooperate with the Spirit in "re-tuning" so that our lives better resonate with the fullness of His Spirit.

As you consider whether your words, thoughts, and actions are in tune with God's Spirit, examine each of the following in the nine-note scale of the Holy Spirit.

Love: "Love is patient, love is kind. Love does not envy, is not boastful, is not arrogant, is not rude, is not self-seeking, is not irritable, and does not keep a record of wrongs. Love finds no joy in unrighteousness but rejoices in the truth. It bears all things, believes all things, hopes all things, endures all things" (1 Cor. 13:4-7).

Joy: "Now may the God of hope fill you with all joy and peace as you believe so that you may overflow with hope by the power of the Holy Spirit" (Rom. 15:13).

Peace: "I have told you these things so that in me you may have peace. You will have suffering in this world. Be courageous! I have conquered the world" (John 16:33).

Patience: "Therefore, brothers and sisters, be patient until the Lord's coming. See how the farmer waits for the precious fruit of the earth and is patient with it until it receives the early and the late rains" (Jas. 5:7).

Kindness: "And be kind and compassionate to one another, forgiving one another, just as God also forgave you in Christ" (Eph. 4:32).

Goodness: "Therefore, as we have opportunity, let us work for the good of all, especially for those who belong to the household of faith" (Gal. 6:10).

Faithfulness: "Whoever is faithful in very little is also faithful in much, and whoever is unrighteous in very little is also unrighteous in much" (Luke 16:10).

Gentleness: "To slander no one, to avoid fighting, and to be kind, always showing gentleness to all people" (Titus 3:2).

Self-control: "Instructing us to deny godlessness and worldly lusts and to live in a sensible, righteous, and godly way in the present age" (Titus 2:12).

Choose one of the nine fruits of the Spirit that God is currently growing within you. Give an example of how you have seen the Spirit changing your thoughts, perspective, attitude, or behavior in that area of your life.

What is one of the characteristics listed in Galatians 5:22-23 that you would like to reflect more in your life? What simple and practical steps could you take this week to cooperate with God in further developing that attribute? (For example, if you would like to grow in patience, you might consider letting cars merge in front of you in traffic or allowing people to move ahead of you in line when you get coffee or at the grocery store.)

SERVING HIS KINGDOM

Disciples serve Jesus by expending time, talents, and resources in His kingdom.

REFLECT

We examined in the previous session how God sent us Jesus to show us the way and then sent believers the gift of the Holy Spirit to help us become the people He created us to be. We saw that it is God's own Spirit that works in and through us to make us more like Jesus. Because of this, we can be encouraged that God's Spirit dwells within us, empowers us, and transforms us to live in tune with God's desires and plans for us.

In this session, we'll take a deeper look at what it means to live and serve as part of God's kingdom.

Which of the assignments did you explore this week? How did it go?

What did you learn or experience while reading the Bible?

What questions would you like to ask?

PRAY

Begin the session by connecting with God through prayer. Use the following guidelines as you speak with Him:

- Ask God to guide your discussion about what it means to serve His kingdom.

- Pray that God would open up our hearts and minds to what it looks like for us to fully invest in building God's kingdom rather than our own kingdoms.

- Thank God that when Jesus returns and establishes His kingdom here, all earthly kingdoms, death, and destruction will be defeated permanently.

- Pray that because of this future hope, it will affect how we serve the kingdom today.

INTRODUCTION

Every street surrounding every new car dealership in America has something in common: every day on that street, tens of thousands of dollars simply vanish. There's no getting around it, stopping it, or avoiding it. The dealerships, the police, and the public haven't been able to do anything about it. So, what's so unique about every street surrounding every new car dealership in America that causes it to hemorrhage money? Depreciation.

On average, every new car that has just been purchased will decline in value approximately 9 percent the moment its new driver takes it off the lot. In other words, every year, roughly 15 million new car owners spend money on something that loses money as quickly as it's spent. This isn't just true with cars. It's true with almost everything we spend money on. Depreciation is an inescapable phenomenon for most purchases. Accountants even have a line item in spreadsheets to track the depreciation of assets for an individual, family business, or for a multi-national corporation. Depreciation is so common that we've even come up with tax incentives where depreciation can be "written off" because it's considered an expense, a cost of life.

There are some objects such as rare cars, unique collectibles, or unusual art that actually increase in value over time. Yet, a rare car could lose value after a hail storm damages it, a rare baseball card could lose value if the player is exposed for a scandal, and a piece of art could lose value if a huge collection from the same artist was discovered nullifying its rarity. Virtually everything we spend money on will either begin depreciating in value immediately or at some point down the road.

However, there is one thing that is guaranteed not to depreciate in value: God's kingdom.

What is your most valuable possession? What makes it valuable?

If you didn't have this thing, how would your life be different? How would not having this effect your eternal existence?

Jesus said that when we expend our lives in God's kingdom, there is nothing that can destroy, diminish, or even steal our investment (see Matt. 6:19-21). In this session we will consider what the kingdom of God is and how we, as disciples, are called to serve as Jesus did by spending our time, talents, energies, and resources in the most rewarding and permanent venture in history: the movement of God's kingdom.

KNOW THE STORY

There is a man in Scripture who is famous for what he held onto and it challenges us still today.

¹⁸ A ruler asked him, "Good teacher, what must I do to inherit eternal life?" ¹⁹ "Why do you call me good?" Jesus asked him. "No one is good except God alone. ²⁰ You know the commandments: Do not commit adultery; do not murder; do not steal; do not bear false witness; honor your father and mother." ²¹ "I have kept all these from my youth," he said. ²² When Jesus heard this, he told him, "You still lack one thing: Sell all you have and distribute it to the poor, and you will have treasure in heaven. Then come, follow me." ²³ After he heard this, he became extremely sad, because he was very rich. ²⁴ Seeing that he became sad, Jesus said, "How hard it is for those who have wealth to enter the kingdom of God! ²⁵ For it is easier for a camel to go through the eye of a needle than for a rich person to enter the kingdom of God." ²⁶ Those who heard this asked, "Then who can be saved?" ²⁷ He replied, "What is impossible with man is possible with God." ²⁸ Then Peter said, "Look, we have left what we had and followed you." ²⁹ So he said to them, "Truly I tell you, there is no one who has left a house, wife or brothers or sisters, parents or children because of the kingdom of God, ³⁰ who will not receive many times more at this time, and eternal life in the age to come."
LUKE 18:18-30

According to Luke's account, this man not only had great wealth, but he was also a moral, religious leader. He had everything—yet his heart was still restless. He appears to be sincere in asking Jesus about the one thing he lacked—eternal life. The assurance of eternal life would have completed his portfolio and his sense of security. Jesus, able to perceive the intentions of this man, cuts to the heart of the matter. Jesus instructs him to do the one thing that he has yet to do: sell everything and give it to the poor so that he can follow Him. Jesus wasn't condemning the wealth of this man but rather was confronting a heart that was wrapped up in his possessions. Sadly, this man walked away, holding onto what he thought was treasure, not allowing his hands and his heart to grasp the true treasure in front of him—Jesus.

Can you relate to this man? What attitudes or fears may have prompted him to choose wealth and a religious life over Jesus?

UNPACK THE STORY

THE KINGDOM OF GOD

At the end of this story in Luke, we see that this rich young ruler served and invested in himself rather than serving the King and investing in His kingdom. In doing so, he missed the chance to hold onto the very thing that would finally fulfill his restless heart.

Share a time when you were faced with a choice to serve yourself or to serve God. What did you give up? What did you gain?

The kingdom of God is an integral truth not only within Jesus' teaching but also within the larger framework of the entire biblical narrative. Scripture also refers to the "kingdom of heaven," the "kingdom of the Lord," the "kingdom of Christ," and simply the "kingdom." These are all just different ways to point to the same thing. Namely, there is an active reign of God that is experienced differently throughout history and throughout the universe. The kingdom of God is wherever and whenever God is acknowledged to rule and reign. We see from Genesis through Revelation amazing examples of God exercising His rule and reign in different ways.

We see from Genesis through Revelation amazing examples of God exercising His rule and reign in different ways.

We see this all the way at the beginning in Genesis when, through the power of God's word, all things in the universe were created, and God described it all as "very good" (Gen. 1:31). In the garden of Eden, we experienced the wholeness that came from God ruling over us. However, we rebelled against God and placed ourselves on the throne of our own hearts. We rejected God as King, and we lost the experience of thriving in God's kingdom. In doing so, human kingdoms were established that were the complete antithesis of the experience of God's kingdom. There was injustice, exploitation, discord, insecurity, and so much more. In contrast, God's reign and rule are unlike any other authority, power, or earthly ruler. Unlike other earthly kingdoms, God's kingdom is marked by peace, joy, love, prosperity, security, and significance among many other things.

When we pray "Your kingdom come" from the Lord's Prayer, what are we essentially asking of God (Matt. 6:10)?

What are some evidences of God's kingdom at work in our lives and in the lives of other disciples around us?

OUR PLACE IN GOD'S KINGDOM

When Jesus came to earth, He inaugurated a new and permanent reality of the kingdom of God. Wherever Jesus went, God's kingdom was experienced. It was an already present reality. Sins were forgiven, the blind received sight, and the sick were miraculously healed. Those on the margins of society were embraced, and even the dead were raised to life. God's reign and rule were active and present in Jesus' life. Furthermore, Jesus invites His followers to be ambassadors and agents for God's kingdom work. We've been invited to experience life with Jesus as King and to serve and invest in God's kingdom, both individually and corporately.

What would it look like for us to invest more fully in building God's kingdom rather than our own kingdoms? Share specific examples of using our time, resources, and skills differently.

Whenever we participate in God's kingdom work by putting into practice Jesus' teaching through the power of the Holy Spirit, we are able to experience the present reality of God being King in our lives. In many ways, the kingdom of God has drastically different values than kingdoms of this world. Enemies are loved, the marginalized are brought in, the meek inherit the earth, the weak members of the community are described as indispensable, and humble service is the greatest display of power. It's no wonder that Jesus says, "seek first the kingdom of God" (Matt. 6:33).

However, there is also a future reality of God's kingdom that has yet to be realized. When Jesus returns and establishes His kingdom here, all earthly kingdoms, death, and destruction will be defeated permanently. What we experience now in regard to living as citizens of heaven is just an appetizer to the brilliant banquet that is our future inheritance as the people of God, living eternally in God's presence in the new heavens and new earth. Because of this future hope, we live differently today. As the apostle Paul wrote in 1 Corinthians 15:58, "Therefore, my dear brothers and sisters, be steadfast, immovable, always excelling in the Lord's work, because you know that your labor in the Lord is not in vain."

We've been invited to experience life with Jesus as King and to serve and invest in God's kingdom, both individually and corporately.

How can a future reality motivate us to give ourselves fully to the work of the Lord today?

ENGAGE

Since Jesus is extravagantly generous and gracious with us, let us follow His model in a tangible way by being generous with others. As a group, decide how you can be Jesus' hands and feet. Use the time remaining to brainstorm ideas to serve the kingdom of God as a group. Don't just talk about it; make a plan to carry it out. Below are some options to get you started.

- Provide meals for someone in need.

- Clean up the yard of a neighbor, a single parent family, or a senior citizen.

- Make lunches for the homeless at your local shelter or food pantry.

- Create a "Serve Day" as a group and find someone in need inside or outside of the church.

- Collect money as a group to help someone who is struggling financially, for a mission trip that someone in the church is raising money for, or for a family seeking support for an upcoming adoption.

PRAYER REQUESTS

In addition to studying God's Word, work with your group leader to create a plan for personal study, worship, and application between now and the next session. Select from the following optional activities to match your personal preferences and available time.

⬆ Worship

☑ Read your Bible. Complete the reading plan on page 70.

☐ Spend time with God by engaging the devotional experience on page 71.

☐ Connect with God each day through prayer asking Him to show you areas in your life that you can give for the sake of the kingdom.

➡⬅ Personal Study

☐ Read and interact with "The Kingdom of God" on page 72.

☐ Read and interact with "Our Place in God's Kingdom" on page 74.

⬅➡ Application

☐ Take some time this week to read and ponder Matthew 13:10-50. Spend time in prayer and journaling, considering the many ways in which our King describes His kingdom.

☐ Consider giving a small sum of money anonymously to someone in need, paying for a student's scholarship for Christian camp, or paying for the food of the car behind you at a fast-food restaurant.

☐ Memorize Matthew 6:33: "But seek first the kingdom of God and his righteousness, and all these things will be provided for you."

☐ Other:

 **WORSHIP**

READING PLAN

Read through the following Scripture passages this week. Use the space provided to record your thoughts and responses.

Day 1
1 Corinthians 15:50-58

Day 2
Mark 10:35-45

Day 3
1 Peter 4:1-11

Day 4
Galatians 5:1-15

Day 5
John 13:12-20

Day 6
Matthew 25:31-46

Day 7
Philippians 2:1-11

"IS LIKE"

The kingdom of God is so expansive and wondrous that Jesus never defined it in a sound bite. Rather, He invited people to have eyes that would see things that only come through faith in Jesus, empowered by the Holy Spirit, as we continually refocus on the things that matter most to Jesus. Of the many ways in which Jesus invited others to see, taste, experience, encounter, and expend their lives on the kingdom of God, one of Jesus' frequent methods was to paint word pictures by telling "is like" stories.

For example, here are a few "is like" stories that help frame our perspective of Jesus' kingdom:

> "The kingdom of heaven is like a man who sowed good seed in his field" (Matt. 13:24, NIV).

> "The kingdom of heaven is like a mustard seed" (Matt. 13:31).

> "The kingdom of heaven is like leaven that a woman took and mixed into fifty pounds of flour until all of it was leavened" (Matt. 13:33).

> "The kingdom of heaven is like treasure, buried in a field" (Matt. 13:44).

> "The kingdom of heaven is like a net that was let down into the lake and caught all kinds of fish" (Matt. 13:47, NIV).

> "The kingdom of heaven is like a king who wanted to settle accounts with his servants" (Matt. 18:23, NIV).

> "The kingdom of heaven is like a landowner who went out early in the morning to hire workers for his vineyard" (Matt. 20:1).

> "The kingdom of heaven is like a king who prepared a wedding banquet for his son" (Matt. 22:2, NIV).

For those looking for a sound bite definition of the kingdom so that it can be quantified and consumed, Jesus' approach is frustrating. And yet, Jesus asks loud enough for us to hear, "With what can we compare the kingdom of God, or what parable can we use to describe it?" (Mark 4:30). It's as if Jesus is inviting us to explore the kingdom with Him. He invites us to experience it and to expend our lives on it. We could spend the rest of our lives exploring it as we put Jesus' teaching into practice and we would still not grasp the fullness of God's kingdom.

THE KINGDOM OF GOD

The concepts of a kingdom and a king are foreign to most of us in the United States. Yet, we have many examples from history and popular culture of kings and kingdoms.

> *In the space below, describe some attributes of a kingdom and some characteristics of a king, both good and bad.*

> *How does this metaphor help you understand God's kingdom and God at work in our world?*

Consider the city in which you live. Could you describe it in one sentence? If you try, what about the restaurants you forgot to mention? What about the mayor who didn't quite make it in the description? How about the parks, the schools, and the residents? What about the street names, the plant names, and the shop names? Did you remember to include the elevation? The population? The average temperature in the summer? You see, to reduce the enormous complexity of even the smallest city into just one simple sound bite is to attempt the impossible.

If instead, you began to experience the city, walk the streets, meet the residents, patronize the shops, eat the food, get lost and ask for directions, sit still as the shadows get longer at the end of the day, walk barefoot across the grass dew in the park at sunrise—then you might get a glimpse of what your city is. Truth be told, a lifetime in a city still isn't enough to grasp the fullness of it.

Infinitely more is the task of grasping the kingdom of God. And yet, Jesus says that children are better equipped at experiencing it (see Mark 10:15). Perhaps there is a sense of awe and wonder that we grow out of as we mature into adulthood that is the necessary variable in experiencing God's kingdom.

What keeps many people from giving themselves fully to serving Jesus, the King of kings?

What choices can you make to serve the kingdom today?

Read each of the following passages and note what each says about the kingdom.

Matthew 6:31-33

John 18:33-38

Luke 17:20-21

There is no greater investment with our time, talents, and treasure than investing in the kingdom of God, "where neither moth nor rust destroys, and where thieves don't break in and steal," and where we find at the center the most valuable treasure of all—Jesus (Matt. 6:20).

OUR PLACE IN GOD'S KINGDOM

Every kingdom has a king. Thankfully, there is none like King Jesus. He is a humble King, a mighty King, a righteous King, a faithful King, a just King, a merciful King, and so much more. The more you get to know Jesus as King, the more you will experience and learn about His kingdom.

We see a glimpse of Jesus as King in Matthew 25, but it may not be what you expect. We find our King identifying Himself with "the least of these"—the hungry, the thirsty, the stranger, the naked, the sick, and the imprisoned.

31 "When the Son of Man comes in his glory, and all the angels with him, then he will sit on his glorious throne. 32 All the nations will be gathered before him, and he will separate them one from another, just as a shepherd separates the sheep from the goats. 33 He will put the sheep on his right and the goats on the left. 34 Then the King will say to those on his right, 'Come, you who are blessed by my Father; inherit the kingdom prepared for you from the foundation of the world. 35 " 'For I was hungry and you gave me something to eat; I was thirsty and you gave me something to drink; I was a stranger and you took me in; 36 I was naked and you clothed me; I was sick and you took care of me; I was in prison and you visited me.' 37 "Then the righteous will answer him, 'Lord, when did we see you hungry and feed you, or thirsty and give you something to drink? 38 When did we see you a stranger and take you in, or without clothes and clothe you? 39 When did we see you sick, or in prison, and visit you? ' 40 "And the King will answer them, 'Truly I tell you, whatever you did for one of the least of these brothers and sisters of mine, you did for me.' 41 "Then he will also say to those on the left, 'Depart from me, you who are cursed, into the eternal fire prepared for the devil and his angels! 42 For I was hungry and you gave me nothing to eat; I was thirsty and you gave me nothing to drink; 43 I was a stranger and you didn't take me in; I was naked and you didn't clothe me, sick and in prison and you didn't take care of me.' 44 "Then they too will answer, 'Lord, when did we see you hungry, or thirsty, or a stranger, or without clothes, or sick, or in prison, and not help you?' 45 "Then he will answer them, 'I tell you, whatever you did not do for one of the least of these, you did not do for me.' 46 "And they will go away into eternal punishment, but the righteous into eternal life."
MATTHEW 25:31-46

Who do you most identify with: the sheep or the goat? Why?

Jesus clearly lays out in this parable how we are to love, care for, and serve one another—especially the disadvantaged. Jesus also doesn't stand back at a distance and give these instructions without first giving Himself as an example. Throughout the New Testament, we find Jesus serving and helping those in need. And He also taught this to His disciples.

> [42] Jesus called them over and said to them, "You know that those who are regarded as rulers of the Gentiles lord it over them, and those in high positions act as tyrants over them. [43] But it is not so among you. On the contrary, whoever wants to become great among you will be your servant, [44] and whoever wants to be first among you will be a slave to all. [45] For even the Son of Man did not come to be served, but to serve, and to give his life as a ransom for many."
> MARK 10:42-45

Jesus models for us a life of constant service to different kinds of people in various types of situations, and He expects the same from us. We love one another because Christ loved us. We serve one another because Christ served us. We sacrifice and die to our comforts and conveniences for the sake of others because Christ sacrificed His life for our sake on the cross.

Are there specific types of people you find easier to serve? What are some types of service that you enjoy providing for others? Explain.

How can you stretch yourself this week by serving outside your comfort zone? Write out a plan below.

SPREADING THE GOOD NEWS

As disciples, we are sent by Jesus to
embody the good news of the gospel
with both our words and our lives.

REFLECT

In Session 5, we discussed what the kingdom of God is and how we, as disciples, are called to serve as Jesus did by spending our time, talents, energies, and resources in the most rewarding and permanent venture in history. Because Jesus models for us a life of constant service to different kinds of people in various types of situations, He expects the same from us. We love one another because Christ loved us. We serve one another because Christ served us. We sacrifice and die to our comforts and conveniences for the sake of others because Christ sacrificed His life for our sake on the cross.

Which of the assignments did you explore this week? How did it go?

What did you learn or experience while reading the Bible?

What questions would you like to ask?

PRAY

Begin the session by connecting with God through prayer. Use the following guidelines as you speak with Him:

- Ask God to give your group the heart to be Great Commission disciple-makers: "Go, therefore, and make disciples of all nations" (Matt. 28:19).

- Pray that even before you begin discussing this session that God would place the names of unbelievers on your hearts and minds.

- Ask God to give each group member the boldness and wisdom to share his or her own story of faith.

- Pray that God will give your group the ears to listen, the hearts to love, the hands to serve, and the words to speak both grace and truth to these people.

INTRODUCTION

Everyone loves to get good news. Whether it is from a friend, spouse, teacher, boss, doctor, or mechanic, good news is always received with a warm welcome. But why is it that the gospel, which literally means "good news," can be so difficult for us to share? Why does it stir up feelings of inadequacy, stress, obligation, anxiety, and fear of rejection? Perhaps we have forgotten that the good news of the gospel is actually the greatest news that has ever been delivered.

What good news have you received recently? What made it good, and how did it impact you?

Sometimes words become so familiar, they lose their meaning, becoming instead an altered, assumed, or powerless term. The word *gospel* is one of those words. If you asked a hundred Christians to explain what *gospel* means, you might get a hundred different answers. In the same way, since "to evangelize" literally means, "to be a messenger of the gospel," you may likely hear many diverse definitions of *evangelism*.

In this session, we will provide a pathway for evangelism that is both narrow and broad. It's narrow because it's only and always about Jesus. It's broad because the good news about the gospel has both personal and cosmic ramifications. Those three words—Jesus, personal, and cosmic—hold together the richness, beauty, and power of the gospel that Jesus has empowered us to embody with our words and our lives. When we allow the good news of the gospel to penetrate deep into our hearts, we are then propelled to share that same good news with others.

How would you define "the gospel" in one sentence?

What thoughts and emotions are stirred up when you hear the word "evangelism"?

KNOW THE STORY

Perhaps one of the most fascinating accounts of evangelism in the Bible is found in Acts 17. Luke records in extraordinary detail how the apostle Paul shared the good news of Jesus to the Greeks in a way that was both personal and cosmic at the same time. As you read this passage, pay attention to details from his description of this scene. Underline words or phrases that either stand out as significant, surprising, or needing further explanation. Then spend some time discussing these things.

22 Paul stood in the middle of the Areopagus and said: "People of Athens! I see that you are extremely religious in every respect. 23 For as I was passing through and observing the objects of your worship, I even found an altar on which was inscribed: 'To an Unknown God.' Therefore, what you worship in ignorance, this I proclaim to you. 24 The God who made the world and everything in it—he is Lord of heaven and earth—does not live in shrines made by hands. 25 Neither is he served by human hands, as though he needed anything, since he himself gives everyone life and breath and all things. 26 From one man he has made every nationality to live over the whole earth and has determined their appointed times and the boundaries of where they live. 27 He did this so that they might seek God, and perhaps they might reach out and find him, though he is not far from each one of us. 28 For in him we live and move and have our being, as even some of your own poets have said, 'For we are also his offspring.' 29 Since we are God's offspring then, we shouldn't think that the divine nature is like gold or silver or stone, an image fashioned by human art and imagination. 30 "Therefore, having overlooked the times of ignorance, God now commands all people everywhere to repent, 31 because he has set a day when he is going to judge the world in righteousness by the man he has appointed. He has provided proof of this to everyone by raising him from the dead."
ACTS 17:22-31

What did you underline or highlight from this passage?
What stood out as significant, surprising, or needing further explanation?

UNPACK THE STORY

EVANGELISM IS NARROW

In light of this passage, let's consider the three words mentioned in the introduction as a way to understand Paul's method of evangelism: Jesus, personal, and cosmic.

Jesus: For Paul, and for us, it's always and only all about Jesus. The gospel is defined entirely by the reality of Jesus' life and work. The fullness of Jesus' life extends all the way back into eternity past (see John 17:1-5), extends into eternity future (see Rev. 21:1-7), and is the subject of the entire Bible.

God's personal and cosmic answer to the question "What is the gospel?" can be summarized in one name: Jesus. He is our only hope to be reconciled to God. Only in Jesus do we find lasting peace, justice, and satisfaction. Through Jesus, we are redeemed, renewed, and restored. And this is why evangelism is narrow—because it's only and always about Jesus.

> Only in Jesus do we find lasting peace, justice, and satisfaction. Through Jesus, we are redeemed, renewed, and restored.

Discuss for a moment some of the things we would miss if we attempted to share the gospel with someone while failing to include Jesus. Why is Jesus so important to this good news?

The apostle Paul was in Athens because the good news about Jesus had completely captured his heart and mind, causing Paul to leave his life of religious legalism and embrace a liberating relationship with God through faith in Jesus. Paul was willing to go to the ends of the earth and endure all things, not to earn God's love but because God's love extended to him through Jesus. Though Paul spent much of his time in Athens talking about a variety of things, the motivation for all of his words was to lead people directly to Jesus.

Who shared the gospel with you? What did they do or say that was persuasive and moved you toward Jesus?

Was there anything they did or said that was unhelpful and moved you away from Jesus? Briefly explain.

EVANGELISM IS BROAD

Evangelism is also broad because the gospel has both personal and cosmic ramifications.

Personal: Acts 17 is just one of many passages that reminds us that the good news of the gospel has personal implications. In fact, the gospel is so personal that it transcends every culture, every nation, every language, and every unique human experience and can be delivered to every person on earth on a first name basis. The life that Jesus lived and the work that He accomplished are not just impersonal loopholes that can get us out of hell if we just believe in Jesus. Rather, the life and work of Jesus were accomplished with us in mind, His cherished children, as well as every other human being.

This is why the apostle Paul starts off by making observations about the lives of those in Athens. He wants to communicate the gospel in words that they would personally understand. Paul even goes so far to quote two poems about the Greek god Zeus as he shares the gospel. Though he uses words he's never used before, he's pointing directly to the same, unchanging Jesus who is the only way to the Father. As a result, at least two individuals, as recorded by Luke, embraced the good news about Jesus that day.

Why is it important to understand the culture, values, experiences, and perspectives of those with whom we are sharing the gospel?

Cosmic: While the good news of the gospel has personal ramifications, it also affects everything in all of creation. Acts 17:24-27 records Paul describing God as the Creator and Sustainer of all things, the Mover of history, and the One who desires people to reach out to Him. The good news of the gospel is twofold: (1) Jesus redeems and reconciles every person who puts his or her faith in Jesus; and (2) Jesus is reconciling and restoring all things on earth and in the heavens. Though Paul delivers the message of the gospel personally to those in Athens, he reminds them that the work God is accomplishing through Jesus is beyond the largest scale imaginable.

The gospel is so personal that it transcends every culture, every nation, every language, and every unique human experience.

In your opinion, why is it so amazing that Jesus longs to redeem, reconcile, and restore us?

ENGAGE

In the space provided below, draw a basic sketch of your street, apartment building, or workplace. Label each house, door, or cubical with the name of the person, or people, who live there. Mark those you know to be followers of Jesus, other religious affiliations, and those who you don't yet know.

Spend some time brainstorming as a group some ideas of how you might share Christ through words or acts of service. For example, you might consider having an "Acts 17 Party" and invite neighbors, coworkers, and friends to a potluck or barbeque with your small group. Inviting these people into your home to hang out with you and your group is a great way for them to experience the love of Christ.

When you are done brainstorming ideas, pair up with one other person in the group. Share the sketch with each other and pray together for God's Spirit to work in you and in each person on the sketch.

PRAYER REQUESTS

....

....

....

....

....

....

....

In addition to studying God's Word, work with your group leader to create a plan for personal study, worship, and application between now and the next session. Select from the following optional activities to match your personal preferences and available time.

⬆ Worship

☑ Read your Bible. Complete the reading plan on page 84.

☐ Spend time with God by engaging the devotional experience on page 85.

☐ Identify three people in your life who you would like to share the good news of Jesus Christ with and pray for each of them that God would give you ears to listen, a heart to love, hands to serve, and words to speak both grace and truth.

➡ ⬅ Personal Study

☐ Read and interact with "The Gospel Always Points to Jesus" on page 86.

☐ Read and interact with "Romans Road" on page 88.

⬅ ➡ Application

☐ Memorize Romans 10:15b: "How beautiful are the feet of those who bring good news."

☐ Pay attention to conversations you have this week. Journal about all of those conversations and how you could transition into the sharing of your faith in each. Attempt to give as many transitions as possible.

☐ Share your faith in Jesus with at least one person this week. This may be intimidating, but remember that you don't need to give a speech or attempt to convince people in any way. You just need to tell your faith story simply and sincerely, with love for the person with whom you share it.

☐ Other:

 **WORSHIP**

READING PLAN

Read through the following Scripture passages this week. Use the space provided to record your thoughts and responses.

Day 1
Romans 10:14-17

Day 2
Matthew 5:13-16

Day 3
Isaiah 6:1-13

Day 4
Matthew 28:16-20

Day 5
Jeremiah 1:4-8

Day 6
Colossians 4:2-6

Day 7
1 Peter 3:13-22

YOUR STORY

The good news of Jesus' life and work is that it has personal ramifications for you, along with everyone else. And though it's easy to forget, you are the world's foremost expert when it comes to describing your life and how you have experienced the good news of Jesus. There is no seminary professor, pastor, teacher, or leader who is more qualified to speak about your life than you are.

In 1 Peter 3:15, you are reminded that you should be "ready at any time to give a defense to anyone who asks you for a reason for the hope that is in you." Consider this an opportunity to get ready for a future moment when you can share your story with someone who is curious about how you have experienced Jesus.

Take some time to put into words how you have experienced this good news so that you can readily share with others when asked about the hope that is in you that flows from a relationship with Jesus. Use the questions below as you craft your story.

How did your relationship with Jesus free you from striving to earn God's approval?

How did Jesus free you from a particular sin or addiction?

How did Jesus change your perspective even though your circumstances stayed the same?

How did Jesus give meaning to your life, give you hope, give you peace, or set you free from the bondage of a guilty conscience?

THE GOSPEL ALWAYS POINTS TO JESUS

If you explored every New Testament account of the disciples of Jesus sharing the good news about Jesus to others, you'd quickly find there is no formulaic speech delivered. In fact, since no two evangelistic accounts are exactly the same, it's a great reminder that the gospel is far more personal than a program. However, every telling of the good news has one thing in common: it always points to Jesus.

Is it reassuring or frustrating to know that there is not a formula for sharing your faith with someone else? Why?

When Peter preached about the good news of Jesus in Acts 2:14-36, he was speaking to a Jewish audience and used language that would be very personal to their history as a nation. He quotes from the Hebrew Scriptures, specifically segments written by Joel and David that point to Jesus. He summarizes everything by saying, "Therefore let all the house of Israel know with certainty that God has made this Jesus, whom you crucified, both Lord and Messiah" (v. 36). As a result, three thousand people came to faith in Jesus and were baptized that day.

With results like that, it might be tempting to think that Peter's message is the formula for evangelism that we should adopt. Quote a little Joel and David, point to Jesus, and tell people to repent and be baptized, and bingo: easy, repeatable evangelism. The problem is this is the only instance where Joel and David are mentioned in all the New Testament accounts of evangelism. The next evangelistic moment in Acts 3:11-26 reveals that Peter, speaking again to the Jewish people, mentions Abraham, Isaac, Jacob, the holy prophets, Moses, and Samuel as he described Jesus as the Holy and Righteous One. At this point, it might be tempting to suggest that evangelism always involves mentioning characters from the Old Testament. However, the next evangelistic account in Acts 4:8-12, records Peter as not mentioning any Old Testament names but rather references a recently healed beggar before concluding, "There is salvation in no one else, for there is no other name under heaven given to people by which we must be saved" (v. 12).

On and on it goes throughout the New Testament. It's always about Jesus, but it's never the same exact words that lead people to Jesus. This required much prayer, which is constantly mentioned as occurring among the early disciples, and it required being led by the Holy Spirit at all times.

Briefly describe how coming to know Jesus was different for you than for others in your family or small group.

The early disciples were being faithful to Jesus' last command to be "witnesses to Jesus" before He ascended to the right hand of God (see John 5:31-47). Knowing they couldn't do this on their own strength or wisdom, Jesus empowered every believer with the Holy Spirit (see Acts 2:4) and sent them out in the same way that God the Father had sent the Son (see John 20:21). This involved the words they spoke and the lives they lived. Their lives were compelling, drawing thousands to follow Jesus, despite tremendous persecution.

As you continue to follow the history of the early church through the Book of Acts and even in the New Testament Letters from Paul and others, you find that evangelism is always and only about Jesus. Luke summarized the disciples' passion in Acts 5:42, "Every day in the temple, and in various homes, they continued teaching and proclaiming the good news that Jesus is the Messiah." At the same time, different words were used to point to Jesus.

- Stephen summarizes much of the Old Testament to point to Jesus (Acts 7:2-53).
- Philip, through the power of the Spirit, healed many paralyzed people to point to Jesus (Acts 8:4-8).
- Peter boldly confronted Simon the sorcerer to point him to Jesus (Acts 8:9-24).
- Philip listened to and had compassion for the Ethiopian eunuch to point him to Jesus (Acts 8:26-40).
- Peter stepped outside his comfort zone to associate with a Gentile to point him to Jesus (Acts 10:25-48).
- Paul and Silas prayed and sang hymns in prison to point to Jesus (Acts 16:25-34).
- Paul reasoned with people in different ways to point to Jesus (Acts 17:1-34).

In summary, what would it look like for us today to point to Jesus everywhere we go? Because there is no formula to follow, we must be obedient by continually putting into practice all that Jesus commanded. The more you cultivate a lifestyle of discipleship, the more equipped you'll be to point to Jesus in your conversations and in your actions.

What one thing can you do this week to share Christ through words or actions?

Think about a specific person in your life with whom God might be leading you to share the good news. What are some fears that have been stopping you? Pray and ask God to give you courage and opportunity to share. Remember it is our job to share the gospel, and it is the Holy Spirit's job to convict, compel, and change hearts.

ROMANS ROAD

One classic way to explain the gospel and God's plan of salvation is known as the "Romans Road." It uses a series of verses from the Book of Romans to explain the path to salvation through Christ. The Bible is clear that it is only through faith in Jesus that we are forgiven and reconciled to God. There are five essential elements of this message. Each of these steps is necessary to understand the one that follows. As you read through these verses, consider how you might explain each of these concepts to someone who is not yet a believer.

Who needs salvation:

> [10] ... There is no one righteous, not even one.
> [11] There is no one who understands;
>   there is no one who seeks God.
> [12] All have turned away;
>   all alike have become worthless.
>   There is no one who does what is good,
>   not even one.
> ROMANS 3:10-12

> For all have sinned and fall short of the glory of God.
> ROMANS 3:23

Why we need salvation:

> For the wages of sin is death, but the gift of God is eternal life in Christ Jesus our Lord.
> ROMANS 6:23

How God provides salvation:

> But God proves his own love for us in that while we were still sinners, Christ died for us.
> ROMANS 5:8

How we receive salvation:

> 9 If you confess with your mouth, "Jesus is Lord," and believe in your heart that God raised him from the dead, you will be saved. 10 One believes with the heart, resulting in righteousness, and one confesses with the mouth, resulting in salvation.
> ROMANS 10:9-10

> For everyone who calls on the name of the Lord will be saved.
> ROMANS 10:13

The result of salvation:

> Therefore, since we have been declared righteous by faith, we have peace with God through our Lord Jesus Christ.
> ROMANS 5:1

> Therefore, there is now no condemnation for those in Christ Jesus.
> ROMANS 8:1

> 38 For I am persuaded that neither death nor life, nor angels nor rulers, nor things present nor things to come, nor powers, 39 nor height nor depth, nor any other created thing will be able to separate us from the love of God that is in Christ Jesus our Lord.
> ROMANS 8:38-39

Which step is the most difficult for you to describe? Explain your answer.

Which step would be the most challenging for your unbelieving friend to understand and accept? Explain your answer.

Where do you think most people in our culture get stuck and reject Jesus?

CHRIST CAME TO US

We are His mission; He is our solution.

REFLECT

In the previous session, we saw that evangelism that is both narrow and broad. It's narrow because it's only and always about Jesus. It's broad because the good news about the gospel has both personal and cosmic ramifications. When we allow the good news of the gospel to penetrate deep into our hearts, we are then propelled to share that same good news with others.

Over the next several sessions, we'll examine our mission as followers of Jesus who live, work, and play in a world that's often opposed to Him. But first let's reflect on your experiences from this past week. Use the following questions to begin this session with discussion.

Which of the assignments did you explore this week? How did it go?

What did you learn or experience while reading the Bible?

What questions would you like to ask?

PRAY

Stop for a moment to pray, either individually or as a group:

- Thank God for your own salvation and for the salvation of your friends and family who have joined you in following Christ.

- Ask Him to fill you afresh with awe and wonder over His gift of salvation.

- Ask God to provide meaningful connections between you and those in your path who have yet to commit their lives to Him.

INTRODUCTION

"Here I come to save the day!"

Do you remember the old *Mighty Mouse* cartoons? The main character was an animated, anthropomorphic mouse in a suit and cape. He had a wide range of powers—flight, super strength, x-ray vision, telekinesis, and more—all of which he used to free victim after victim from the clutches of evil foes.

Each time Mighty Mouse achieved victory over his adversary, an unseen audience would erupt in loud applause as orchestral music played in the background. Then the narrator would say, "What a mouse. *What* a mouse!"

Who were some of your favorite heroes growing up?

What powers or characteristics in these heroes did you appreciate most?

Most people enjoy hero stories. Whether real or imagined, we appreciate the thought of someone powerful coming to the rescue of those in need. We're also grateful for the compassion, or even the sense of duty, that would compel one person to help another.

Perhaps what we like best about hero stories, however, is the way rescue always seems to occur just in the nick of time. Can you picture that moment in your mind? The situation is grim. The forces of evil are on the cusp of accomplishing their goals, and the very lives of innocent people are about to be thrown away.

Then, right at the moment when the last of our hope slips away, we hear it: "Here I come to save the day!" Salvation has come.

This session is a reminder that all of us who have trusted in Christ have experienced that moment. When humanity was hopelessly snared in sin—when we had no hope of pulling ourselves away from the forces of evil inside our own hearts—God sent His Son to meet our most pressing need.

Christ came to us with a mission, and He has won the day.

KNOW THE STORY

In today's culture, we're often tempted to think of the Christmas story as a self-contained event. We celebrate the birth of Jesus, but we don't always remember that He was born with a purpose. Christ came on a mission to save us from our sin.

[18] The birth of Jesus Christ came about this way: After his mother Mary had been engaged to Joseph, it was discovered before they came together that she was pregnant from the Holy Spirit. [19] So her husband Joseph, being a righteous man, and not wanting to disgrace her publicly, decided to divorce her secretly.

[20] But after he had considered these things, an angel of the Lord appeared to him in a dream, saying, "Joseph, son of David, don't be afraid to take Mary as your wife, because what has been conceived in her is from the Holy Spirit. [21] She will give birth to a son, and you are to name him Jesus, because he will save his people from their sins."

[22] Now all this took place to fulfill what was spoken by the Lord through the prophet:

> [23] See, the virgin will become pregnant
> and give birth to a son,
> and they will name him Immanuel,

which is translated "God is with us."

[24] When Joseph woke up, he did as the Lord's angel had commanded him. He married her [25] but did not have sexual relations with her until she gave birth to a son. And he named him Jesus.
MATTHEW 1:18-25

What thoughts or memories come to mind when you read these verses? Why?

UNPACK THE STORY

SALVATION COMES THROUGH A PERSON

We can't properly appreciate the concept of salvation until we think deeply about the Person of Jesus Christ. Why? Because Jesus is more than the One who accomplished our salvation; He's not simply the Being who made salvation possible.

Instead, Jesus *is* our salvation.

When you embraced the call to follow Christ, you didn't respond to a concept or a message. You responded to a Person. You followed Jesus—the same Jesus who was born of a virgin, grew, learned, lived, and died almost 2,000 years ago. The same Jesus who is Lord of God's kingdom and Master of your life.

When you consider your coworkers, friends, and family members who have not yet experienced salvation, you want that to change. You want them to experience the joy that comes with the forgiveness of sin—and that's good. That's natural. But they won't experience that joy by better understanding a doctrine or by reciting a prayer.

They need to meet Jesus. They need to experience Him.

> When you embraced the call to follow Christ, you didn't respond to a concept or a message. You responded to a Person.

What do you remember about the first time you encountered Jesus in a personal way?

When was the last time you enjoyed a personal encounter with Jesus?

The Gospel writers understood the importance of Jesus' existence as a living, breathing Person. That's why Matthew made a point of starting his record of Jesus' life by writing about His miraculous birth. Luke did the same. And John opened his Gospel with a similar truth expressed in a more abstract form: "The Word became flesh and dwelt among us" (John 1:14a).

How does Jesus' Personhood help you follow Him?

SALVATION COMES WITH A PLAN

The message of the gospel is simple: By sending Jesus to us, God made a way where there was no way. God has a plan of rescue for all humanity. God's plan is not just a good plan, or even the best of many plans—it's the *only* plan sufficient to meet the most pressing need in our lives: the need to be rescued from our sin.

We've seen that salvation is anchored in the Person of Jesus Christ. But simply knowing who Jesus is and what He's done isn't enough to actually accomplish the forgiveness of our sins. God's plan involves each person encountering Jesus in a way that leads to a relationship with Him.

And still there's more. Once we encounter Jesus, we must respond to Him with faith, which is an act of the will in which we place our trust in Him.

What are some common misconceptions about salvation?

To think about salvation in another way, God's plan requires that all people:

- **Realize:** The first step in being rescued is to realize we're in trouble. God's plan is for everyone to realize that they're not sufficient to save themselves—that Jesus is the only way of rescue from the corruption of sin.

- **Repent:** Once we realize our situation, we must repent. To repent involves being genuinely sorry for sin. It means changing our minds about our behavior and actively turning away from sin and toward God.

- **Receive:** Salvation comes as an offer—a gift—of God's grace. And that gift must be accepted as an act of faith.

These concepts may seem basic, but it's vital to have a firm foundation as we continue to explore our mission as disciples of Jesus.

> Once we encounter Jesus, we must respond to Him with faith, which is an act of the will in which we place our trust in Him.

How can we help others recognize and follow these steps?

ENGAGE

To live as a disciple of Jesus means joining Him in accomplishing His mission for the world. As we'll see throughout this study, we have a part to play in helping others recognize the reality of their sin and turn to Jesus for salvation. Sometimes that part includes directly sharing the gospel message. Other times our contributions are more subtle.

For example, prayer is one of the most important things we can do for those who have yet to experience salvation in Christ.

Make a list of at least five people in your spheres of influence who are not yet disciples of Jesus. Commit to praying daily for each of these people by name. Ask God to send His Spirit and convict them of their sin.

1.

2.

3.

4.

5.

PRAYER REQUESTS

....

....

....

....

....

....

....

....

In addition to studying God's Word, work with your group leader to create a plan for personal study, worship, and application between now and the next session. Select from the following optional activities to match your personal preferences and available time.

⬆ Worship

☑ Read your Bible. Complete the reading plan on page 98.

☐ Connect with God each day through prayer.

☐ Spend time with God by engaging the devotional experience on page 99.

➡ ⬅ Personal Study

☐ Read and interact with "Identifying with Jesus" on page 100.

☐ Read and interact with "Preparing to Be a Witness" on page 102.

⬅ ➡ Application

☐ Make an effort to deepen your relationship with an acquaintance this week. Seek out someone you'd like to know better and start a conversation.

☐ Memorize Luke 19:10: "For the Son of Man has come to seek and to save the lost."

☐ Continue praying daily for the people in your life who need to experience salvation. Seek opportunities to speak with these people in meaningful ways—and especially keep an eye open for chances to share the gospel message.

☐ Dig deeper into the doctrine of salvation by listening to a podcast on that subject from a respected teacher. You could also read a book, listen to a sermon, or study an article.

☐ Other:

 **WORSHIP**

READING PLAN

By describing the earliest days of the church, the Book of Acts offers helpful information and inspiration for joining God in His mission. Use the space provided to record your thoughts and responses as you read.

Day 1
Acts 1:1-14

Day 2
Acts 1:15-26

Day 3
Acts 2:1-36

Day 4
Acts 2:37-47

Day 5
Acts 3:1-26

Day 6
Acts 4:1-22

Day 7
Acts 4:23-37

THE WORD

The central truth of this resource is that God came to earth with a mission to redeem His people through the forgiveness of their sins and that He has called His followers—those who've already experienced forgiveness—to participate in that mission. This is the gospel, the good news.

As you contemplate the gospel and prepare to engage in the mission of sharing that truth with others, remember that everything begins and ends with Jesus. He is the embodiment of the gospel. He is the Word made flesh, as the apostle John reminded us:

> The Word became flesh
> and dwelt among us.
> We observed his glory,
> the glory as the one and only Son from the Father,
> full of grace and truth.
> JOHN 1:14

Jesus is God and was God from "the beginning" (John 1:1). He is God the Son, the second Person of the Trinity. Remaining God, not becoming anything less than fully God or anything other than God, Jesus took on human flesh. Why did He do this? Because all flesh was corrupt. Only a complete and perfect sacrifice could satisfy forever God's righteous requirement for justice against sin (see Rom. 3:25).

At the same time, Jesus exists as a man. He came into the world as a baby, born of a virgin (see Matt. 1:18-25; Luke 1:26-38). Jesus lived a span of decades as a person and experienced life as we do. Fully identifying Himself with us, He experienced the normal process of growth and development. He encountered the full breadth of human experiences: heat and cold, hunger and thirst, work and rest.

Jesus had to be made like us in all things in order to qualify as the substitute for our sins—and to help us when we're tested (see Heb. 2:17-18). He was one with us in every way, except that He did not sin. Jesus lived a perfect life and offered Himself as a sacrifice in order to save us from our sins.

What have you learned about Jesus through your own experiences?

How would you like to experience Jesus in the days and years to come?

IDENTIFYING WITH JESUS

Here's a truth that's worth repeating: Jesus didn't come to earth simply to secure our salvation; He *is* our salvation. His mission involved making Himself available to all people as the solution to our primary problem. He came so that we could believe in Him and therefore receive forgiveness from our sin.

As we saw in Matthew 1:18-25, the way Jesus came into our world was totally unique in the scope of history. While any other king would have been born in a palace, Jesus was born in a stable. While any other king's coming would have been heralded throughout the kingdom and widely publicized to all available subjects, the announcement of Jesus' birth was given only to a few humble witnesses (see Matt. 1:20-23; Luke 1:26-35; Luke 2:9-14). While other children are given names that shape who they will become, the name given to Jesus declared who He already was.

Given the uniqueness of Jesus' incarnation, it's no surprise that people reacted in a number of different ways to His presence in the world.

Read the following passages of Scripture and record the different ways people responded to Jesus.

Matthew 2:1-12

Matthew 2:13-18

Luke 2:8-20

Luke 2:36-38

Luke 4:16-30

As disciples of Jesus, we are called to participate in His mission to redeem the world. We have experienced Christ as our salvation, and therefore we work to help others experience Him as well. Yet, we must understand that joining Jesus in His mission means we will encounter a number of different reactions and responses, as He did.

There will be times when people respond to your work with joy. They will see your actions and hear as you proclaim the gospel, and they will be glad. They will welcome you into their lives even as they welcome Christ into their hearts.

There will be other times, however, when people respond to your work in negative ways, including bitterness, scorn, anger, and even rage. When you join Jesus in His mission to redeem the world, you will experience strife and strain in your relationships, both personal and public. You will experience persecution in different forms. You will be confused at times, frustrated and angry at other times.

And Jesus knew all of this when He called you to follow Him:

> ¹⁸ "If the world hates you, understand that it hated me before it hated you.
> ¹⁹ If you were of the world, the world would love you as its own. However, because you are not of the world, but I have chosen you out of it, the world hates you. ²⁰ Remember the word I spoke to you: 'A servant is not greater than his master.' If they persecuted me, they will also persecute you. If they kept my word, they will also keep yours."
> JOHN 15:18-20

When have you experienced negative interactions or negative emotions in your efforts to follow Jesus?

What rewards have you experienced while participating in Jesus' mission for the world?

Jesus encountered trouble as He worked to redeem the people of this world. We will encounter the same. Yet, by following His example—by modeling His courage and reflecting His resolve—we can continue to persevere as disciples of Christ on a mission in our world.

PREPARING TO BE A WITNESS

The Bible teaches that there is no hope for anyone who doesn't believe and receive God's plan of salvation by accepting Jesus Christ. Think deeply about that for a moment. In the world today there are really only two groups of people: those who are saved and those who are lost. Yet, the wonderful news of the gospel is that Jesus came to save us all. Through a step of faith, the fate of lost people can be changed forever.

Those of us who have been rescued and reconciled to God have been entrusted with the message of salvation (see Matt. 28:18-20) and the ministry of reconciling others to Him (see 2 Cor. 5:18-20). How do we do that? Where should we start? How do we ready ourselves to be instruments for reconciling others to God?

Here are a few ideas to begin preparing yourself for life as a witness to God's plan of salvation.

1. Memorize and meditate on the Scriptures. Apart from knowing the Savior ourselves, there is little else that helps our confidence as witnesses more than knowing God's Word. Memorize a few verses and passages that explain what salvation is and why we need it. This discipline helps us be ready to share the truth whenever or wherever an opportunity presents itself.

If you're new to Bible memorization, the following Scripture passages are a great place to start:

- Romans 3:23-24
- Romans 5:8
- Romans 6:23
- Romans 10:9-10

What Bible verses will you memorize in the coming weeks?

2. Move toward unsaved people. Jesus came to seek and save the lost, which means He sought to encounter them. He looked for ways to engage with them. Likewise, we should look for opportunities to develop relationships with unsaved people. Grocery store clerks, neighbors, homeless people, barbers, coworkers, coaches—all who are not yet following Christ—these make up our mission field. Consider ways you can get to know these individuals in your sphere of influence in order to impact their spiritual condition.

As you identify people who need to experience Jesus as their salvation, be proactive in deepening those relationships. Pursue them with love, friendship, and patience. Knowing the lost people in your community will help you understand how to share with them in a way that intersects with their lives.

Which people in your life need to experience salvation? Make a list.

3. Make prayer for lost people a priority. When we pray for those who need salvation, we stand as intercessors between God and them, seeking for God to come closer to them and them to come closer to God. As we plead for God's intervention in the lives of lost people, He begins to work in their hearts. Not only that, He also begins to sensitize our hearts to the point where we share His burden for them.

No one wants the lost to be saved more than God. By seeking Him, He also opens our eyes to opportunities to share with them.

Commit to praying each day for the people on your list (above).

4. Prepare your personal testimony. The story of what Christ has done for you personally is one of the greatest tools you have for leading others to an awareness of the Lord's calling on their lives. When people see and hear you, they encounter living proof of the power of Christ to save a soul and transform a life.

It's important that you're able to share your testimony in a concise, straight-to-the-point manner. Perhaps the simplest way to be sure that what you share is clear and concise is to write it out. Doing so helps make a long story short. And committing your testimony to memory helps you be able to share it whenever or wherever an opportunity arises.

How would you describe your testimony? See if you can record it in the space below.

CHRIST CAME WITH A MISSION

Jesus came to serve God and set us free.

REFLECT

In the previous session, we focused on Jesus' presence in this world. We know from God's Word that Jesus left heaven and entered our world in a physical way—an event we often refer to as the incarnation. We also reinforced the truth that Jesus is our only hope for salvation. He is the only solution to the problem of our sin.

As you prepare to dig deeper into the mission at the core of Jesus' incarnation, take a moment to reflect on your experiences in recent days.

Which of the assignments did you explore this week? How did it go?

What did you learn or experience while reading the Bible?

What questions would you like to ask?

PRAY

Stop for a moment to pray, either individually or as a group:

- Thank God for actively engaging in His mission to redeem the world.

- Ask Him to come alongside those who are not saved and to help them become free from their sin and spiritual blindness.

- Ask for wisdom and clarity of mind as you study God's Word in your group and throughout the coming week.

INTRODUCTION

The Secret Millionaire is a reality TV series in which super-wealthy individuals live undercover for a week in an impoverished or deprived community. The millionaires willingly volunteer to leave their homes, conceal their identities, and deny themselves the privileges of fortune in order to live in poverty.

Having physically relocated to a neighborhood in need, the millionaires share the living conditions of their new neighbors by taking residence in a local housing project and cutting themselves back to welfare-level wages. They intentionally connect with the community by living among the people and identifying with their experiences. Their nearness allows them to observe real life and real situations. It also provides opportunities to connect with their neighbors' struggles, share in their distresses, and grieve their lack of basic necessities.

Watching and listening, the millionaires consider what could be done to relieve the suffering around them and improve the lives of their new neighbors. On the last day before returning to paradise, the millionaires reveal their true identities and surprise a person or group of people with a generous endowment from their own fortunes.

How would you describe the way you feel when you're able to help someone?

What are some of the more significant needs in your church congregation? Your community?

The Secret Millionaire offers a great example of how an empathetic presence, generous provisions, and empowered people can help make tough circumstances better. It also offers a helpful reminder of what Jesus did—and is still doing—for all of us.

God sent His one and only Son into the world to bring lasting solutions to the lingering problems of others. He came to both to save and to serve.

KNOW THE STORY

It's often difficult to explain biblical concepts in a short and simple way. That's true today, and it was also true in the early church. That's one of the reasons Christians have treasured the following verses from the Book of Philippians. Known as the "Hymn to Christ," this passage captures both Jesus' identity and His mission in the world:

⁵ Adopt the same attitude as that of Christ Jesus,

> ⁶ who, existing in the form of God,
> did not consider equality with God
> as something to be exploited.
> ⁷ Instead he emptied himself
> by assuming the form of a servant,
> taking on the likeness of humanity.
> And when he had come as a man,
> ⁸ he humbled himself by becoming obedient
> to the point of death—
> even to death on a cross.
> ⁹ For this reason God highly exalted him
> and gave him the name
> that is above every name,
> ¹⁰ so that at the name of Jesus
> every knee will bow—
> in heaven and on earth
> and under the earth—
> ¹¹ and every tongue will confess
> that Jesus Christ is Lord,
> to the glory of God the Father.
> PHILIPPIANS 2:5-11

What's your initial reaction to verse 5?

How do these verses contribute to your understanding of Jesus' mission in our world?

UNPACK THE STORY

CHRIST CAME TO SERVE GOD

There's a common misconception regarding the reasons for Jesus' presence in our world. Specifically, many people believe humanity was the driving force behind the incarnation—that Jesus came to us simply because we needed Him so desperately.

It's certainly true that humanity needed Christ, and still needs Christ. We are hopeless without Him. Yet, it's important to understand that *God* was the primary motivation for Jesus' incarnation. Not us.

In Philippians 2:6-7, Paul reinforced the truth that Jesus is God. The Son has always existed "in the form of God." However, in order to accomplish God's mission to redeem the world, Jesus willingly "emptied himself" in order to take on the form of man. Specifically, Paul said Jesus became "a servant"—but not to us. Jesus didn't bend His will to accommodate the desires of people. Rather, Jesus willingly emptied Himself in order to serve God. Verse 8 continues the same idea. By humbling Himself, Jesus was obedient to God's will, over and above our needs.

As disciples of Jesus, then, we're called to the same mission and carry the same purpose—to serve God and honor Him.

Why is it dangerous to believe Jesus' mission was based exclusively on our needs?

Jesus confirmed His own motivations while speaking to the crowds:

> For I have come down from heaven, not to do my own will, but the will of him who sent me.
> JOHN 6:38

Jesus understood that His mission was to serve God and glorify Him. It's great news for us that by doing so, He became our salvation. As disciples of Jesus, then, we're called to the same mission and carry the same purpose—to serve God and honor Him. And, as we'll see throughout this study, one of the ways we serve and honor God is by actively serving as a witness to others.

On a practical level, what does it mean to serve God?

CHRIST CAME TO SET US FREE

Here's another misconception regarding Jesus' mission in our world: that it all began at Christmas. Many people believe that Jesus' birth was the start of God's mission to save humanity from our sins.

Instead, the incarnation was a crucial event in the middle of God's larger plan to set humanity free from the bondage of sin—a plan that stretched all the way back to those first moments after Adam and Eve were exiled from the garden of Eden (see Gen. 3:20-24).

Read the following verses and describe how each one illustrates God's plan to rescue people from their sin.

Genesis 12:1-3

Isaiah 53:7-12

Jeremiah 31:31-34

Jesus is our salvation, which means He is our only hope to experience freedom in a spiritual sense. Jesus' death and resurrection are the only door through which we can pass to receive forgiveness and spiritual life. Yet, spiritual freedom isn't the only type of freedom Jesus offers those who will follow Him. He can also set us free from our fears and our doubts. He can set us free from emotions that overwhelm us. He can set us free from physical or financial burdens that weigh us down. He can even set us free from the need to control every aspect of our lives and to solve our problems in our own strength—if we let Him.

In short, Jesus can unshackle us from lives focused on temporary struggles and set us free to participate in the glorious unfolding of God's mission for the world.

> Jesus' death and resurrection are the only door through which we can pass to receive forgiveness and spiritual life.

In what ways have you experienced freedom in Christ?

Of course, when Jesus sets us free, He also calls us to serve as both witnesses and neighbors to those still stuck in the bondage of their sin.

ENGAGE

When people talk about joining Jesus in His mission for the world, they often use the phrase "sharing the gospel." But what is the *gospel,* specifically? How would you define that term?

In a broad sense, the gospel is everything related to the Person and work of Jesus. This includes everything leading up to His birth, His life, His death, and His resurrection—not to mention all of the benefits believers experience as a result. In a more narrow sense, the gospel refers to the "good news" that all people can be saved from the bondage of their sins through the death and resurrection of Christ.

To "share the gospel" then is simply to talk about that good news. And contrary to the opinions of many, there is no "absolutely right" or "correct" way to do so. Just look at the Scriptures!

Read the following passages of Scripture. Compare and contrast each of the different methods used to share the gospel.

Acts 2:14-40

Acts 8:26-35

Acts 17:16-31

PRAYER REQUESTS

....

....

....

....

....

....

....

....

In addition to studying God's Word, work with your group leader to create a plan for personal study, worship, and application between now and the next session. Select from the following optional activities to match your personal preferences and available time.

⬆ Worship

☑ Read your Bible. Complete the reading plan on page 112.

☐ Connect with God each day through prayer.

☐ Spend time with God by engaging the devotional experience on page 113.

➡ ⬅ Personal Study

☐ Read and interact with "Christ Calls Us to Serve God" on page 114.

☐ Read and interact with "Christ Calls Us to Serve Others" on page 116.

⬅ ➡ Application

☐ Pray daily for a person or a group of people in your community who are in need of help—spiritual, financial, or otherwise.

☐ Memorize Mark 10:45: "For even the Son of Man did not come to be served, but to serve, and to give his life as a ransom for many."

☐ As part of your devotional life this week, make a special effort to connect with God as your Master and King. Pray, read the Scriptures, and obey God's commands with the mind-set of a servant.

☐ Go out of your way to serve someone this week. Buy coffee for someone who looks cold. Help clean up your coworker's office. Babysit children for a young couple. Do something kind simply to bless someone you know.

☐ Other:

 # WORSHIP

READING PLAN

Continue exploring the Book of Acts throughout this week. Use the space provided to record your thoughts and responses as you read.

Day 1
Acts 5:1-16

Day 2
Acts 5:17-42

Day 3
Acts 6:1-15

Day 4
Acts 7:1-36

Day 5
Acts 7:37-60

Day 6
Acts 8:1-25

Day 7
Acts 8:26-40

KEEP IT SIMPLE

As human beings, and even as disciples of Jesus, we have a natural tendency to overthink matters that are actually quite simple. Such was the case with the scholar who approached Jesus in Luke 10:

> ²⁵ Then an expert in the law stood up to test him, saying, "Teacher, what must I do to inherit eternal life? "
>
> ²⁶ "What is written in the law?" he asked him. "How do you read it?"
>
> ²⁷ He answered, "Love the Lord your God with all your heart, with all your soul, with all your strength, and with all your mind;" and "your neighbor as yourself."
>
> ²⁸ "You've answered correctly," he told him. "Do this and you will live."
>
> ²⁹ But wanting to justify himself, he asked Jesus, "And who is my neighbor?"
> LUKE 10:25-29

This "expert in the law" was probably a scribe by trade. He may have also served as a Pharisee or teacher of the law. In any event, he approached Jesus with a question that was common among scholars of his day. He wanted to find out Jesus' position on a theological issue in much the same way that a modern politician might ask, "Are you a Democrat or a Republican?"

When Jesus gave his own question back to him, the scholar gave the correct answer. Jesus agreed with him, but that wasn't enough. The scribe wanted to keep going deeper, more complex. He asked, "And who is my neighbor?"

Read Luke 10:30-37 to see Jesus' answer. What strikes you as most interesting about this parable?

Based on this parable, how would you define your neighbors?

Notice the lawyer emphasized who should be the object of love and service, while Jesus emphasized the action itself. Through His parable, Jesus expressed the necessity for less assessment and more action. Moving forward, then, perhaps "Who is my neighbor?" isn't a question we should worry about today. Perhaps we should be asking, "Whose neighbor am I?"

CHRIST CALLS US TO SERVE GOD

When we read through the Scriptures, we find a number of concepts and situations that were common in ancient times but are uncommon today. Think of kings, for example. As modern readers of the Bible, we can recognize the concept of a king on an intellectual level. However, in an era of democracy, it's difficult to really understand what it must have been like to live under the complete, all-powerful rule of a single person.

The same thing is true for the concept of servanthood. As modern readers, we can understand the definition of a *servant* as someone who serves others. However, we typically think of this service in terms of a job. Meaning, the servant serves his or her master for a certain period of time—8 or 10 hours each day, for example—and then "clocks out" to return home and enjoy some rest and relaxation.

In reality, servants in the ancient world were entirely dedicated to meeting the needs and wants of their masters at all times. In fact, it may help us understand things better if we think of the word *slave* instead of *servant*.

> *Read the following passages of Scripture and record what they teach about life as a servant (or slave) in the ancient world.*
>
> *Genesis 16:1-6*
>
>
>
> *Exodus 21:20-21*
>
>
>
> *Deuteronomy 15:12-18*
>
>
>
> *Ephesians 6:5-9*

Why is this important? Because when we accept the call to follow Jesus as His disciples, we are accepting His call to live as servants (or slaves) of God.

As we saw in the group discussion, Jesus Himself came to earth in obedience and service to God. He emptied Himself and assumed "the form of a servant" (Phil. 2:7). As disciples of Jesus, we model Him in all things. Our goal is to become more like Him in every area of life (see 2 Cor. 3:18). Therefore, we follow Christ by joining Him as servants of God.

Sadly, too many Christians believe that serving God is a part-time occupation. When we focus on spiritual things several times throughout our day, we feel justified in pursuing our own interests and desires for the remainder of each day. Again, we often treat serving God as a 9 to 5 occupation, when in reality our identities as disciples of Jesus require a 24/7 commitment.

Jesus Himself made it clear that our service to God must be all-encompassing:

> [7] "Which one of you having a servant tending sheep or plowing will say to him when he comes in from the field, 'Come at once and sit down to eat'? [8] Instead, will he not tell him, 'Prepare something for me to eat, get ready, and serve me while I eat and drink; later you can eat and drink'? [9] Does he thank that servant because he did what was commanded? [10] In the same way, when you have done all that you were commanded, you should say, 'We are worthless servants; we've only done our duty.' "
> LUKE 17:7-10

What's your initial reaction to these verses? Why?

Do you feel you should be rewarded whenever you obey God by doing something positive or rejecting something negative? Explain.

Jesus has called us to serve God, just as He serves and obeys the Father in all things. The wonderful news is that such service is not a burden or a shackle. Instead, only by fully embracing our identities as servants of God can we experience the fullness of life God designed us to enjoy.

CHRIST CALLS US TO SERVE OTHERS

Jesus came to earth with a mission. Though He is God, He willingly emptied Himself in order to enter our world and fulfill that mission, thus serving the Father. As disciples of Jesus, we're also called to serve God, and we're also called to do so by joining Jesus in accomplishing His mission.

Given these truths, it's logical to ask, "What *is* the mission?" What is it we're supposed to aim for or accomplish when we become disciples of Christ? Interestingly, Jesus provided some clear answers to that question when He first announced His ministry (and mission) in a public way:

16 He came to Nazareth, where he had been brought up. As usual, he entered the synagogue on the Sabbath day and stood up to read. 17 The scroll of the prophet Isaiah was given to him, and unrolling the scroll, he found the place where it was written:

> 18 The Spirit of the Lord is on me,
> because he has anointed me
> to preach good news to the poor.
> He has sent me
> to proclaim release to the captives
> and recovery of sight to the blind,
> to set free the oppressed,
> 19 to proclaim the year of the Lord's favor.

20 He then rolled up the scroll, gave it back to the attendant, and sat down. And the eyes of everyone in the synagogue were fixed on him. 21 He began by saying to them, "Today as you listen, this Scripture has been fulfilled."
LUKE 4:16-21

In what ways did Jesus fulfill the prophecy from Isaiah?

How do these verses help you understand your responsibilities as a disciple of Christ?

Jesus alone could fulfill the spiritual implications of Luke 4:16-21. Through His death and resurrection, He proclaimed good news to those in spiritual poverty, freedom for those held captive to sin, life to those oppressed by the law, and sight to those blind to their own need for salvation.

Still, we can join Jesus in His mission on a practical level. Specifically, we can be:

- **God's messengers.** Jesus shared the good news of the gospel with clarity and variety. He communicated in ways that were mindful of the personalities of individual hearers, relevant to their culture, and sensitive to their needs (see John 3:1-16; 4:3-26; Mark 10:21-22). Likewise, serving God faithfully requires us to be competent, creative, and confident messengers of His salvation. We are called to spread the good news.

- **God's ministers.** Throughout His ministry, Jesus took notice of those who needed help. His mission was primarily spiritual, yet He still took the time to focus on physical needs and earthly troubles. He ministered to the poor, the captives, the blind, and the oppressed—and He has called us to do the same.

- **God's missionaries.** Just as Jesus left paradise in order to save us, we are called to go out of our comfort zones in order to make a difference in the world. This may mean going out into our neighborhoods, going out into our country, or going out across the world. The key is obedience to God's leading and a willingness to go in order to serve those in need.

In what situations do you feel most confident about sharing the gospel?

When you think about people with practical needs, who comes to mind?

Where is God calling you to go in order to serve Him and others?

Jesus met the spiritual and physical needs of those He encountered and those He sought out. As His disciples, we are called to do the same.

CHRIST CAME TO DIE

Jesus came to suffer and to sacrifice—

and to call us to do the same.

REFLECT

In the previous session, we took a deeper look at Christ's mission in our world. We saw that He became the salvation for humanity—not in service to humanity, but in service to God. We also learned that Jesus calls us to follow His example by living as servants of God, and that part of our service to God involves intentionally serving other people in order to continue advancing His mission in the world.

As you prepare to engage the climax of Jesus' mission in this world—His death as a sacrifice for the forgiveness of our sin—use the following questions to reflect on your experiences in recent days.

Which of the assignments did you explore this week? How did it go?

What did you learn or experience while reading the Bible?

What questions would you like to ask?

PRAY

Stop for a moment to pray, either individually or as a group:

- Thank God for not withholding any good thing from you, including Jesus.

- Praise God for His plan to make salvation available to all people through the death and resurrection of Jesus.

- Ask God to give you a fresh perspective on suffering and a ready heart to make whatever sacrifices He calls you to make for His glory and for the good of others.

INTRODUCTION

"It was the best of times, it was the worst of times."

The first sentence of Charles Dickens's *A Tale of Two Cities* is one of the most famous opening lines in Western literature, and rightfully so. However, the popularity of that first sentence sometimes overshadows the broader story of the book—a story that is worth remembering because of its striking picture of self-sacrifice for the benefit of others.

Set in London and Paris, the central characters in the book are Charles Darnay and Sydney Carton. Those two men are nearly twins in terms of their physical appearance; yet, they are vastly different on the inside. Darnay is a man of integrity and impeccable character, while Carton is a sly and sarcastic reprobate who drinks too much.

During the story, both men fall in love with Lucie Manette, who represents the ideal woman of her time. Not surprisingly, Lucie chooses to marry Darnay, although Carton becomes a family friend. After years of a peaceful life in London, Darnay is arrested in Paris at the height of the French Revolution because of sins committed by his aristocratic family. He is sentenced to death by guillotine.

At the last moment, however, Carton sneaks into Darnay's prison and knocks him unconscious. Carton arranges to have Darnay smuggled back to London while he remains in prison to ensure his rival's return to Lucie. The next day, Carton is executed in Darnay's place. Carton himself delivers the last line of the book, which is as poignant and powerful as the first: "It is a far, far better thing that I do, than I have ever done; it is a far, far better rest that I go to than I have ever known."[1]

What are some stories from modern culture that reflect the value of self-sacrificial love?

When have you benefited from another person's sacrifice?

Sydney Carton's sacrifice is a moving picture of redemption—a sinful man who willingly died in order to make up for his wasted life. As we'll see in this session, Jesus' sacrifice was something different. In Christ, we see a perfect man who willingly died in order to save the sinful lives of everyone else.

KNOW THE STORY

The truth that Jesus is both fully God and fully human is a foundational doctrine of the Christian faith. And yet it's often hard to imagine Jesus as a genuine human being. It's difficult to think of Jesus, our Lord, encountering such human experiences as loneliness, rejection, and physical pain.

Yet, the Scriptures teach us that Jesus indeed suffered the indignities associated with human life—even the ultimate indignity of physical death.

20 "But you," he asked them, "who do you say that I am?" Peter answered, "God's Messiah."

21 But he strictly warned and instructed them to tell this to no one, 22 saying, "It is necessary that the Son of Man suffer many things and be rejected by the elders, chief priests, and scribes, be killed, and be raised the third day."

23 Then he said to them all, "If anyone wants to follow after me, let him deny himself, take up his cross daily, and follow me. 24 For whoever wants to save his life will lose it, but whoever loses his life because of me will save it. 25 For what does it benefit someone if he gains the whole world, and yet loses or forfeits himself? 26 For whoever is ashamed of me and my words, the Son of Man will be ashamed of him when he comes in his glory and that of the Father and the holy angels. 27 Truly I tell you, there are some standing here who will not taste death until they see the kingdom of God."
LUKE 9:20-27

What questions come to mind when you read these verses?

Make a list of the promises contained in these verses. Which promises strike you as most significant?

UNPACK THE STORY

JESUS SUFFERED

We know from Scripture that Jesus experienced physical suffering on the cross as a necessary part of reconciling humanity with God. Yet, it's also important to recognize the many additional forms of suffering Jesus endured on our behalf:

- **Jesus suffered loneliness.** Jesus was alone in an environment hostile to His way of thinking and contrary to His spiritual composition. He was different from everyone around Him, including His immediate family.

- **Jesus suffered anonymity.** He spent the first 30 years of His life under the radar, unnoticed, uncelebrated, and overlooked by His community (see Mark 6:4). His choice to suffer anonymity can only truly be appreciated when viewed in light of the exaltation He rightly deserved as God.

- **Jesus suffered rejection.** Throughout His public ministry, people threatened Jesus, attempted to bully Him, and even drove Him from their communities. At the end of that ministry, Jesus was abandoned by His closest friends and murdered by the very people He had come to save.

- **Jesus suffered scorn.** Jesus was criticized, accused of demonic activity, slandered, plotted against, interrogated, mocked, spat upon, slapped, wrongfully accused, and beaten to an inch of His life. He was insulted even on the cross as He endured the onset of death. Yet, He did not retaliate against evil people or return their harsh words.

Jesus demonstrated His power by passing through His suffering in victory—and His example inspires us to strive for the same.

How do you respond to the knowledge that Jesus suffered in these ways and more?

What impact does Jesus' suffering have on your life?

Jesus was never granted a pass from suffering. He endured all the pain and indignity common to human life in our world, not to mention the spiritual torment included with carrying the full weight of our sin. Yet, Jesus demonstrated His power by passing through His suffering in victory—and His example inspires us to strive for the same.

JESUS SACRIFICED

The symbol of the cross can mean different things to different people. For some, the cross is an offense—a symbol of a religion they choose to deny. Others see it as a sign of rescue or redemption. Still others as a memorial or symbol of loss.

For any person alive during Jesus' day, the cross was nothing but an instrument of shame, torture, and execution. For Jesus specifically, the cross wasn't just a painful and humiliating responsibility; it was a sentence of ultimate sacrifice—a sentence He willingly chose to carry in unfettered, unflinching obedience to the Father.

Jesus made two foundational choices in His obedience to God. And as you seek to live as Christ's disciple in this world, you must make those choices as well.

First, you must choose to deny yourself. To deny yourself means to give up or surrender all you have and all you are to Jesus. Human management is certain to get in the way of divine ownership. Therefore, living as a disciple of Christ means continually choosing to set aside or even abandon your plans, your interests, your desires, your hopes, and your dreams in order to follow His plans and His interests in the world.

Where do you often experience dissonance between your desires and God's plans?

Second, you must choose to take up your own cross. While the cross was once a symbol of death, it now points to Jesus' faithful execution of God's will. Jesus made a willing sacrifice. As His disciple, you must make the same sacrifice. Having set aside control of your own life, you must take up whatever work Jesus calls you to perform.

Jesus made a willing sacrifice. As His disciple, you must make the same sacrifice.

How would you describe the work Jesus has called you to do?

Disciples of Jesus must deny themselves and take up their crosses. In what ways have you engaged these crucial choices in your own life?

ENGAGE

Many Christians are comfortable with the theory of surrendering to God or submitting to His will. We understand why we should surrender, and we agree that submission is important. But we sometimes forget that genuine submission involves a conscious act. *Surrender* is a verb.

In other words, in order to deny ourselves and take up our crosses, we must actually do something.

Use two or three minutes of private reflection to think about an action or step you can take to intentionally submit yourself to God's will.

As a group, recite Psalm 37:5-9 as a way of affirming your commitment to surrender.

> 5 Commit your way to the LORD;
> trust in him, and he will act,
> 6 making your righteousness shine like the dawn,
> your justice like the noonday.
>
> 7 Be silent before the LORD and wait expectantly for him;
> do not be agitated by one who prospers in his way,
> by the person who carries out evil plans.
>
> 8 Refrain from anger and give up your rage;
> do not be agitated—it can only bring harm.
> 9 For evildoers will be destroyed,
> but those who put their hope in the LORD
> will inherit the land.
> PSALM 37:5-9

PRAYER REQUESTS

....

....

....

....

1. Charles Dickens, *A Tale of Two Cities* (Mineola, NY: Dover Publications, 1999), 1 and 293.

In addition to studying God's Word, work with your group leader to create a plan for personal study, worship, and application between now and the next session. Select from the following optional activities to match your personal preferences and available time.

⬆ Worship

☑ Read your Bible. Complete the reading plan on page 126.

☐ Connect with God each day through prayer.

☐ Spend time with God by engaging the devotional experience on page 127.

➡ ⬅ Personal Study

☐ Read and interact with "Jesus Calls Us to Suffer" on page 128.

☐ Read and interact with "Jesus Calls Us to Sacrifice" on page 130.

⬅ ➡ Application

☐ Throughout the week, ask God to reveal any subtle rebellion or attitude in your life that may be keeping you from total submission to Him. Ask for forgiveness and cleansing (see 1 John 1:8-9).

☐ Memorize Philippians 1:29: "For it has been granted to you on Christ's behalf not only to believe in him, but also to suffer for him."

☐ Be intentional about seeking joy this week. Even as you consider your sufferings in light of the gospel, choose to also enjoy the blessings God has given you.

☐ Be intentional about blessing others this week as well. Keep an eye open for those who are in the middle of suffering, and take action to demonstrate kindness.

☐ Other:

 # WORSHIP

READING PLAN

Continue exploring the Book of Acts throughout this week. Use the space provided to record your thoughts and responses as you read.

Day 1
Acts 9:1-19

Day 2
Acts 9:20-43

Day 3
Acts 10:1-16

Day 4
Acts 10:17-48

Day 5
Acts 11:1-18

Day 6
Acts 11:19-30

Day 7
Acts 12:1-25

OUR FRIEND IN SUFFERING

It sounds strange to say, but we receive many blessings because of the suffering Jesus endured. Obviously, the most important of those blessings is being offered a chance to experience forgiveness for our sins and enjoy reconciliation with God in this life—not to mention the promise of eternal life in heaven during the life to come.

But we should not overlook the additional blessings that Jesus' suffering provides us. For example, the fact that Jesus experienced the full breadth of life in our world means He is familiar with everything we experience in our own lives. He can sympathize with our struggles.

That's one of the primary messages in the Book of Hebrews:

> 14 Therefore, since we have a great high priest who has passed through the heavens—Jesus the Son of God—let us hold fast to our confession. 15 For we do not have a high priest who is unable to sympathize with our weaknesses, but one who has been tempted in every way as we are, yet without sin. 16 Therefore, let us approach the throne of grace with boldness, so that we may receive mercy and find grace to help us in time of need.
> HEBREWS 4:14-16

> 7 During his earthly life, he offered prayers and appeals with loud cries and tears to the one who was able to save him from death, and he was heard because of his reverence. 8 Although he was the Son, he learned obedience from what he suffered. 9 After he was perfected, he became the source of eternal salvation for all who obey him.
> HEBREWS 5:7-9

Take a moment to pray and thank Jesus for the suffering He endured on your behalf.

As you contemplate the reality of Jesus' suffering, allow yourself to be vulnerable and honest about your own struggles. Ask for guidance on how to continue living for God's glory even during suffering.

JESUS CALLS US TO SUFFER

It's important to understand that disciples of Jesus haven't cornered the market on suffering. All people suffer. And yet it is true that Christians should differ from the rest of the world in terms of their response to suffering. While many people suffer hopelessly, desperately, or bitterly, Christians suffer purposefully.

Specifically, we suffer for the spread of the gospel and for the advancement of good.

> *How have your responses to suffering changed throughout the different phases of your life?*

The apostle Paul is perhaps the greatest example we have in the Bible of suffering for the spread of the gospel. Paul's writings proclaim to believers of all ages that not only have we been given the glorious gift of belief in Christ, but we've also been endowed with the privilege of suffering for Him (see Phil. 1:29). While we never suffer to redeem the world—that's already been accomplished by Christ—we do suffer as part of our efforts to reach the world with the gospel message.

> *Read the following passages of Scripture and record what they teach about suffering for the spread of the gospel.*
>
> *Philippians 3:7-9*
>
> *Colossians 1:24-26*
>
> *2 Timothy 1:8-12*

Paul was willing to go anywhere and to suffer any persecution for the privilege of sharing God's message about Christ. For this Paul was beaten, stoned, shipwrecked, imprisoned, sleep deprived, hungry, thirsty, cold, and without adequate clothing (see 2 Cor. 11:24-28). Eventually, he was martyred.

Read Philippians 1:12-18. How would you summarize Paul's conclusions about his own suffering?

When Paul wrote the Book of Philippians, he was a prisoner in Rome. He'd been labeled as a criminal, and he knew such a label could cause others to feel ashamed of him or withdraw from him—or worse, withdraw from active participation in the church.

Paul wanted the church at Philippi to have the proper perspective on the trouble he was experiencing. It wasn't something to be ashamed of or discouraged about. He wanted them to know not only that God was at work in the circumstance of his incarceration, but *how* God was at work. He wanted them to understand how God uses our sufferings—the dangerous, stressful, heartbreaking, and life-threatening circumstances in our lives—to spread the gospel to those who don't know Him and to strengthen others who would become more emboldened to speak up about Him.

God can also use your suffering as a means to bring about good in your life and in the lives of others. We don't always like to think about it, but it's true. Whatever God allows to come upon you, He also determines what its use will be in drawing others to Himself and His purposes. The circumstances in your life that have hindered you, bothered you, or frustrated you may actually be magnifying His presence and power in the eyes of those surrounding you. Knowing that doesn't make those circumstances any more fun, but it can help you endure suffering with purpose and resolve.

When have you seen personal suffering result in something good?

Read Philippians 1:21-30. What principles does Paul offer in these verses for enduring suffering with purpose?

As we live out our faith to the best of our abilities, we will experience suffering. Yet, we need not be broken or crushed by the weight of that suffering. Through God's power, we can endure it. Better still, we can live purposefully in the knowledge that our suffering may be used by God to spread the message of the gospel and to advance the cause of good in this world.

JESUS CALLS US TO SACRIFICE

There's no way to avoid the truth: Living as disciples of Jesus will require us to make sacrifices. And let's be clear, we're not talking about vague or general sacrifices, such as giving up the pleasure of immorality or releasing the opportunity to be filthy rich. Instead, the sacrifices we make to follow Jesus will be both real and concrete.

> *Read the following passages of Scripture and record what they teach about making sacrifices in order to follow Christ.*

> *Matthew 10:37-39*

> *Matthew 16:24-27*

> *Luke 9:57-62*

> *Luke 14:31-33*

Let's dig deeper into the specific types of sacrifices required to follow Jesus.

First, followers of Jesus must sacrifice possessions. While God does not forbid us from having things, He does want to be sure that *things* don't have *us*. To ensure that God has first place in our hearts, we must untie our affections from the things we own. We must be able to part with material possessions and wealth whenever God leads us to do so.

> *What are some of your most prized possessions?*

Next, followers of Jesus must sacrifice relationships. God will have no rivals for our affections. If we're ever forced to choose between honoring God and honoring our loved ones, we must be ready to choose God unequivocally. Those who would stand in the way of God's interests in our lives or try to discourage us from obeying Him are to be denied the authority to dictate our direction. God is our most sacred relationship, and God alone.

> *What symptoms indicate that one of your personal relationships is taking precedence over your relationship with God?*

In addition, followers of Jesus must sacrifice their plans. There will be times when following Christ requires us to sacrifice our plans in favor of God's plans. He reserves the right to change any of our plans, including our family plans, vacation plans, education plans, retirement plans, financial plans, and even our lunch plans. Followers of Christ humbly allow God to order their steps, giving Him authority over every plan (see Jas. 4:13-15). We submit our intentions to Him each day, surrender our way of doing things to His way, and submit our ambitions and future goals to Him.

> *How will you intentionally submit your short-term and long-term plans to God?*

Finally, followers of Jesus must sacrifice their positions. Surrendering position means being ready to descend from whatever rank we think we've achieved or rise from whatever rest we think we've earned in order to fulfill God's present agenda. It involves relinquishing any honor or role we have, instead yielding to Christ who is to be honored above us (see John 3:30). It involves refusing to use our God-given role in the body of Christ or our social status for personal advantage, but only for the public good as a servant to others (see Luke 22:27).

> *What steps can you take to prepare yourself for any change of position, location, or status that God may require of you?*

WE DIE WITH CHRIST

Death to self is the first step in following Jesus.

REFLECT

In the previous session, we explored the amazing truth that Jesus willingly suffered and sacrificed Himself in order to provide a way for humanity to experience reconciliation with God. We also saw that choosing to follow Jesus as His disciples means embracing our own calls to suffer and sacrifice—all in service of proclaiming the message of the gospel and advancing God's kingdom in this world.

As you begin this session, be ready for a switch in focus. We've seen that Christ came to us, that He came with a mission, and that He willingly came to die on our behalf. In the next three sessions, we'll take a deeper look at what it means for us to follow a similar pattern.

Which of the assignments did you explore this week? How did it go?

What did you learn or experience while reading the Bible?

What questions would you like to ask?

PRAY

Stop for a moment to pray, either individually or as a group:

- Take a moment to reflect silently on your experiences in recent weeks. Share with God what you've learned about yourself and about His Word.

- Thank God for the chance to connect with Jesus and the reality of His sacrifice through your own experience of dying to self.

- Ask the Holy Spirit to reveal anything that might be hindering your walk with the Lord Jesus Christ.

INTRODUCTION

How often do people think about death? Or, how often should people think about death? The answer to those questions can change based on your perspective.

When you think about it from a personal point of view, death is a once-in-a-lifetime experience. All people die, of course, but we only experience death once—and only at the very end of our lives. Therefore, many people rarely think about death. It seems so far off.

When you think about these questions from a global point of view, however, death may seem very near. After all, more than 150,000 people die every day around the world—and more than 50 million people die each year. So, it may also be natural for people to think about death all the time.

How often do you think about death?

What emotions do you typically experience when you think about death?

Strangely enough, it makes sense for disciples of Jesus to think about death more than others in the world. That's because death is exactly what it costs to follow Christ. For some, death will mean physical death—being martyred for the cause of Christ.

But for all, the cost of following Jesus involves death to self. As we saw in the previous session, we must lay down control of our lives in order to take up our crosses and follow Christ. We must sacrifice our own plans and priorities in order to follow and obey Him as our Lord.

As we'll see in this session, our experience of dying to self is both a one-time phenomenon and an ongoing requirement.

KNOW THE STORY

Luke records in chapter 14 of his Gospel that large crowds were following Jesus seemingly for the wrong reasons. They had been amazed by His miracles—feeding the multitudes, healing the sick, casting out demons, and so on—but they weren't fully committed to His mission. That's when Jesus gave them something new to think about:

25 Now great crowds were traveling with him. So he turned and said to them: 26 "If anyone comes to me and does not hate his own father and mother, wife and children, brothers and sisters—yes, and even his own life—he cannot be my disciple. 27 Whoever does not bear his own cross and come after me cannot be my disciple.

28 "For which of you, wanting to build a tower, doesn't first sit down and calculate the cost to see if he has enough to complete it? 29 Otherwise, after he has laid the foundation and cannot finish it, all the onlookers will begin to ridicule him, 30 saying, 'This man started to build and wasn't able to finish.'

31 "Or what king, going to war against another king, will not first sit down and decide if he is able with ten thousand to oppose the one who comes against him with twenty thousand? 32 If not, while the other is still far off, he sends a delegation and asks for terms of peace. 33 In the same way, therefore, every one of you who does not renounce all his possessions cannot be my disciple."
LUKE 14:25-33

How might you have reacted if you heard these words as part of the crowd following Jesus?

How would you summarize Jesus' statements in verses 28-32?

UNPACK THE STORY

DEATH TO SELF IS NECESSARY

It seems to be human nature to react negatively when people demand us to do something. We naturally rebel or resist when given orders. Instead, we prefer a situation where our needs and desires are met first. Even then, we like to be asked nicely. If those conditions are met, and if we're asked in a manner acceptable to us, we'll consider it.

This is not the way of Jesus. In fact, the only thing Jesus wants from us is everything. Notice Jesus' three uses of the word *cannot* in Luke 14:

In order to follow Christ, you must be willing to die to self so that you can live for Him.

- *"If anyone comes to me and does not hate his own father and mother, wife and children, brothers and sisters—yes, and even his own life—he cannot be my disciple" (v. 26).* This is a comparative phrase that basically means our love and devotion to Christ comes absolutely first and above any other human relationship. Our allegiance to Christ makes any other allegiance utterly insignificant.

- *"Whoever does not bear his own cross and come after me cannot be my disciple" (v. 27).* What does it mean to bear your own cross? Very simply it means that you must die to self. Jesus died on the cross for us, and in order to truly follow Him we must follow Him in that death. We must die to our desires, plans, and priorities.

- *"In the same way, therefore, every one of you who does not renounce all his possessions cannot be my disciple" (v. 33).* This is not a comparative analogy. This is not symbolism. When you follow Jesus, you own nothing and possess nothing—except Jesus.

What questions or concerns come to mind when you read the above list? Why?

How should the above verses influence our daily routines as followers of Christ?

In order to follow Christ, you must be willing to die to self so that you can live for Him. This is the foundation for life as His disciple.

DEATH TO SELF BRINGS LIFE IN CHRIST

There are really two ways we experience death as followers of Jesus. The first is the death of our "old selves":

> ¹⁹ For through the law I died to the law, so that I might live for God. ²⁰ I have been crucified with Christ, and I no longer live, but Christ lives in me. The life I now live in the body, I live by faith in the Son of God, who loved me and gave himself for me.
> GALATIANS 2:19-20

This death is what we often refer to as *salvation*. It's a one-time event through which we become a "new creation" (2 Cor. 5:17). The old is gone, and the new has come. Not surprisingly, this form of dying is the simpler of the two.

What benefits have you experienced through the process of dying with Christ?

The second way we experience death as followers of Jesus is through the process of dying to self. And *process* is an important word because—unlike the experience of being born again as a new creation—dying to self is not a one-time event. As we've already seen, it's a life-long journey that involves letting go of our plans, priorities, and possessions.

To put it another way, dying to self is the daily discipline of releasing control of our lives and submitting to the control of Christ.

Dying to self is the daily discipline of releasing control of our lives and submitting to the control of Christ.

Do you agree that the one-time event of dying with Christ is simpler than the ongoing process of dying to self? Explain.

How have you experienced the struggle of dying to self?

In a strange twist, our experiences with death as followers of Jesus aren't negative or morbid in any way. In fact, dying with Christ and daily dying to ourselves are key landmarks on the pathway toward new life.

ENGAGE

In some ways, the concept of "dying to self" is an abstract one. We don't typically wake up in the morning and say: "I'm going to work on dying to self throughout the day. I'll start right after breakfast." Instead, we participate in the process of dying to self through several personal disciplines that help us relinquish control of our schedules, our resources, our priorities, and so on.

As a group, spend a few minutes reviewing the following spiritual disciplines. Use these questions to help spark discussion for each discipline: 1) How would you describe your experiences with this discipline? 2) How does this discipline help you die to self?

Prayer

Reading God's Word

Fasting

Journaling

Solitude

Keeping the Sabbath

Tithing

PRAYER REQUESTS

....

....

....

....

....

....

....

In addition to studying God's Word, work with your group leader to create a plan for personal study, worship, and application between now and the next session. Select from the following optional activities to match your personal preferences and available time.

⬆ Worship

☑ Read your Bible. Complete the reading plan on page 140.

☐ Connect with God each day through prayer.

☐ Spend time with God by engaging the devotional experience on page 141.

➡ ⬅ Personal Study

☐ Read and interact with "Dying to Self Clarifies Our Priorities" on page 142.

☐ Read and interact with "Dying to Self Prepares Us to Go on Mission" on page 144.

⬅ ➡ Application

☐ Start a journal entry this week to record moments when you are confronted with your "old self." Note the different triggers and temptations that make it necessary to once again die to self.

☐ Memorize 2 Corinthians 5:17: "Therefore, if anyone is in Christ, he is a new creation; the old has passed away, and see, the new has come!"

☐ Make a list of spiritual goals for the coming month. What are you hoping to achieve or accomplish as part of your new life in Christ?

☐ Look for opportunities to be vulnerable with others regarding your "old self" and old mistakes. There is no need to flaunt the past, of course, but our honesty can often help those who believe disciples of Jesus are required to be perfect.

☐ Other:

WORSHIP

READING PLAN

Continue exploring the Book of Acts throughout this week. Use the space provided to record your thoughts and responses as you read.

Day 1
Acts 13:1-41

Day 2
Acts 13:42-52

Day 3
Acts 14:1-28

Day 4
Acts 15:1-41

Day 5
Acts 16:1-24

Day 6
Acts 16:25-40

Day 7
Acts 17:1-34

BURIED WITH HIM IN BAPTISM

From the earliest days of the church, the ritual of baptism has served as a way for disciples of Jesus to publicly proclaim their faith in Christ as both Savior and Lord. This is a vital practice that should be undertaken by all Christians after their salvation in obedience to the Scriptures. For example:

> [19] Go, therefore, and make disciples of all nations, baptizing them in the name of the Father and of the Son and of the Holy Spirit, [20] teaching them to observe everything I have commanded you. And remember, I am with you always, to the end of the age.
> MATTHEW 28:19-20

Baptism is also a perfect picture of what it means to die to self—and a reminder for us to engage in that practice daily:

> [1] What should we say then? Should we continue in sin so that grace may multiply? [2] Absolutely not! How can we who died to sin still live in it? [3] Or are you unaware that all of us who were baptized into Christ Jesus were baptized into his death? [4] Therefore we were buried with him by baptism into death, in order that, just as Christ was raised from the dead by the glory of the Father, so we too may walk in newness of life.
> ROMANS 6:1-4

Who among your friends and family would benefit from obeying the Scriptures by becoming baptized?

How can you take full advantage of the baptism services in your church as times to worship God?

What do you appreciate most about the chance to "walk in newness of life"?

DYING TO SELF CLARIFIES OUR PRIORITIES

What's your main priority in life? Followers of Jesus know that God *should* be their primary priority, but it's always helpful to review the recent trajectory of your life and make sure that is the case.

For example, have you funneled a great deal of your time and energy into acquiring money? Or possessions? Do you often dream about achieving fame—or idolize those who have achieved it? Have you based your concept of self-worth on another human being? Or on your position or status as a professional? Do you strive for power or spend a lot of energy seeking to be in control? All of these have proven effective in usurping God's place as the primary priority in our lives.

How would you describe your primary goal or priority in recent months?

What are some signs or symptoms that appear in your life when you begin drifting away from God as your main priority?

As we've seen throughout this session, regaining a focus on dying to self is an excellent way to elevate God and His kingdom as our primary focus. The Scriptures also make it clear that dying to self is a necessary element in moving away from the sinful habits and patterns described above:

> [2] Set your minds on things above, not on earthly things. [3] For you died, and your life is hidden with Christ in God. [4] When Christ, who is your life, appears, then you also will appear with him in glory. [5] Therefore, put to death what belongs to your earthly nature: sexual immorality, impurity, lust, evil desire, and greed, which is idolatry. [6] Because of these, God's wrath is coming upon the disobedient, [7] and you once walked in these things when you were living in them. [8] But now, put away all the following: anger, wrath, malice, slander, and filthy language from your mouth. [9] Do not lie to one another, since you have put off the old self with its practices [10] and have put on the new self. You are being renewed in knowledge according to the image of your Creator.
> COLOSSIANS 3:2-10

What's your initial reaction when reading this passage?

What are some habits or practices that need to be "put to death" in your everyday life?

What are some habits or practices that help you "put on the new self"?

Before Christ, you did what you wanted. Before Christ, you traveled where you wanted. Before Christ, you made the final decisions in every aspect of your life—or at least you thought you did. Now that you've experienced Christ, you have a new Master. And the consistent call from Scripture is that you embrace His authority to set the plan for your life.

Read the following passages of Scripture and record what they teach about the process and benefits of dying to self.

Romans 12:1-2

Galatians 5:22-26

2 Timothy 2:8-13

To follow Jesus as Lord means that we die to everything we want and seek to discover and obey everything He wants. It means Christ has the final say in the affairs and direction of our lives. He is our Savior, and He is our Lord because ultimately He is the King of kings and Lord of lords.

DYING TO SELF PREPARES US TO GO ON MISSION

Take a moment to review some of the major themes you've covered in the last few sessions:

- **Session 7:** Jesus Christ is our salvation. His disciples serve as witnesses to that salvation.
- **Session 8:** Jesus came to serve God and set us free. Jesus calls us to serve God and serve others.
- **Session 9:** Jesus suffered and sacrificed. Jesus calls us to suffer and sacrifice for others.

You can see the pattern that's been developing. Whenever God reaches into our world to bless us in some way, He calls us not to hoard that blessing, but to extend it outward to others.

What are some of the primary ways God has blessed you?

What steps have you taken to extend those blessings to others?

The same principle holds true for the blessing (and responsibility) we've described in this session as dying to self. We've seen that dying to self helps us maintain our focus on God and keep Him as our primary priority. The apostle Paul reminded us of that truth in the Book of 2 Corinthians:

> 14 For the love of Christ compels us, since we have reached this conclusion: If one died for all, then all died. 15 And he died for all so that those who live should no longer live for themselves, but for the one who died for them and was raised.
> 2 CORINTHIANS 5:14-15

How do these verses connect with the concept of dying to self?

But we must remember that the purpose of dying to self goes beyond simply our own benefit. Indeed, when we set ourselves in line with God, we join Him in His mission to redeem the world. Look at how Paul continued his train of thought:

¹⁶ From now on, then, we do not know anyone from a worldly perspective. Even if we have known Christ from a worldly perspective, yet now we no longer know him in this way. ¹⁷ Therefore, if anyone is in Christ, he is a new creation; the old has passed away, and see, the new has come! ¹⁸ Everything is from God, who has reconciled us to himself through Christ and has given us the ministry of reconciliation. ¹⁹ That is, in Christ, God was reconciling the world to himself, not counting their trespasses against them, and he has committed the message of reconciliation to us. ²⁰ Therefore, we are ambassadors for Christ, since God is making his appeal through us. We plead on Christ's behalf: "Be reconciled to God."

2 CORINTHIANS 5:16-20

Make no mistake: dying to self *is* an incredible blessing. Have you considered what a privilege it is to live as a "new creation" (v. 17)? To know that your old self has "passed away" and that "the new has come"? You have been reconciled to God! You are part of His kingdom once again.

Therefore, take pains to prevent yourself from hoarding that blessing.

As disciples of Jesus Christ, God has given us "the ministry of reconciliation" (v. 18). Of course, we don't have the ability or the authority to reconcile people to God—only He can accomplish that. Yet, He has enlisted us to help in the process by serving as agents of the gospel. To use Paul's phrasing, we are "ambassadors for Christ" who have a specific role in proclaiming the good news of salvation. "We plead on Christ's behalf, 'Be reconciled to God'" (v. 20).

How confident do you feel in your role as an ambassador for Christ?

1	2	3	4	5	6	7	8	9	10
Not confident									Very confident

What specific steps can you take to be more active in proclaiming the gospel message this week?

WE GO WITH CHRIST

Jesus sends us out as disciples in
order to make disciples.

REFLECT

In the previous session, we explored the necessary practice of dying to self as a follower of Jesus. We saw that death to self means setting aside our priorities, plans, dreams, and desires—all for the sake of taking Jesus' priorities, plans, dreams, and desires as our own. We also learned that death to self is both a one-time event and a daily discipline.

In this session, we'll take a deeper look at our mission as followers of Jesus.

Which of the assignments did you explore this week? How did it go?

What did you learn or experience while reading the Bible?

What questions would you like to ask?

PRAY

Stop for a moment to pray, either individually or as a group:

- Thank God that He has blessed with you a mission and a purpose that carry weight, both in this world and in the next.

- Ask the Holy Spirit to give you eyes to see the world like He sees the world.

- Proclaim your willingness to serve on mission as an ambassador for Jesus Christ.

INTRODUCTION

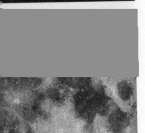

On September 12, 1962, President John F. Kennedy delivered a landmark speech at Rice University in Houston, during which he reminded his listeners about the American goal to land a man on the moon and return him safely. Here's part of what the president said:

> We choose to go to the moon. We choose to go to the moon in this decade and do the other things, not because they are easy, but because they are hard, because that goal will serve to organize and measure the best of our energies and skills, because that challenge is one that we are willing to accept, one we are unwilling to postpone, and one which we intend to win ... It is for these reasons that I regard the decision last year to shift our efforts in space from low to high gear as among the most important decisions that will be made during my incumbency in the office of the Presidency.[1]

This decision to go to the moon required enormous sacrifice, hard work, and courage. At its peak, the Apollo program employed hundreds of thousands of people and required the support of thousands more industrial firms and universities. In financial terms, it cost the U. S. government more than $25.4 billion to land the first astronauts on the moon.[2]

And it worked. On July 20, 1969, the mission was completed when Neil Armstrong stepped off the lunar lander and announced, "That's one small step for man ... one giant leap for mankind." The mission motivated and guided a nation to accomplish something that is still amazing even by today's standards.

In your opinion, what are some of the most impressive accomplishments in human history?

The right mission can inspire people in amazing ways and motivate them to go above and beyond in completing whatever tasks they receive. President Kennedy's mission sparked the imagination and the perspiration of an entire country.

Yet, even that remarkable achievement of human effort pales in comparison to the mission Jesus has given His disciples.

KNOW THE STORY

The Bible records Jesus' mission in several passages, many of which we've explored throughout this resource. In each case, it's clear that Jesus' mission offers a worthy and inspirational vision for His followers—one that will require enormous sacrifice, hard work, and courage on our part.

The most famous expression of Jesus' mission can be found at the end of Matthew's Gospel in some of Jesus' final words to His disciples. Verses 18-20 are called "the Great Commission":

16 The eleven disciples traveled to Galilee, to the mountain where Jesus had directed them. 17 When they saw him, they worshiped, but some doubted.

18 Jesus came near and said to them, "All authority has been given to me in heaven and on earth. 19 Go, therefore, and make disciples of all nations, baptizing them in the name of the Father and of the Son and of the Holy Spirit, 20 teaching them to observe everything I have commanded you. And remember, I am with you always, to the end of the age."
MATTHEW 28:16-20

Take note of verse 17. When have you doubted or been confused by your place in Jesus' mission?

What helps you feel confident about Jesus and His mission?

This was the mission statement that guided a group of ordinary, untrained men as they launched the church and laid a foundation for success from which we still benefit today. Yet, this mission wasn't delivered *only* to the disciples of Jesus' day. The above verses also describe our primary mission as followers of Christ within the modern church.

In other words, these verses are a critical summary of your mission as an individual disciple of Jesus Christ.

UNPACK THE STORY

JESUS' MISSION IS ACCOMPLISHED

We saw back in Session 8 of this resource (see page 116) that Jesus began His public ministry by announcing the major points of His mission for the world. Jesus shocked the people of His hometown by proclaiming Himself as the Messiah and promising good news and freedom from suffering to all who needed it.

Look at Luke 4:16-20. How has your understanding of Jesus' mission developed throughout this study?

There is a sense, then, in which Jesus' mission for the world has already been accomplished. In obedience to the Father, Jesus came into our world not only to preach the good news and teach people about the kingdom of heaven, but ultimately to offer Himself as a sacrifice for the atonement of our sins.

> On the cross, Jesus finished what He came to do.

That mission is over. On the cross, Jesus finished what He came to do:

> When Jesus had received the sour wine, he said, "It is finished." Then bowing his head, he gave up his spirit.
> JOHN 19:30

Yet, there is also a sense in which Jesus' mission is still ongoing. There is still work to be done—still people across the world yearning for freedom and release from suffering. More importantly, there are still people who need to hear the good news of the gospel, understand that news, and take action to accept the gift of forgiveness offered to them.

That's where we come in:

> Jesus said to them again, "Peace to you. As the Father has sent me, I also send you."
> JOHN 20:21

When have you felt most passionate about evangelism?

OUR CONTINUING MISSION IS CRITICAL

When we explore the Great Commission verse-by-verse, we find three important truths that guide our mission as followers of Christ:

1. Our mission is to make disciples. Don't miss the primary command in Jesus' commission: "Go, therefore, and make disciples of all nations ..." (Matt. 28:19). Our first step in making disciples is to "go" and engage the world, rather than sitting back and waiting for the world to come to church. There are no set rules for what it means to "make disciples," but the process does involve proclaiming the gospel, baptizing those who follow Christ, and continually teaching them what it means to live as His disciples.

2. Our mission is based on Jesus' authority. Jesus' first declaration to His disciples was critical: "All authority has been given to me in heaven and on earth" (v. 18). We don't make disciples because it's the right thing to do, or even because we want people to go to heaven. Instead, we make disciples because Jesus—the Lord, Master, and King of all the universe—has commanded us to do so.

3. Our mission includes Jesus' presence. Many people overlook verse 20 when they reference the Great Commission, but Jesus' final words are crucial: "And remember, I am with you always, to the end of the age." Not only do we engage our mission under Christ's authority, but also within His presence. We're not called to go it alone or left to figure things out for ourselves. Instead, we have the privilege of daily encounters with Jesus even as we work to achieve the mission He gave us.

How would you describe what it means to "make disciples"?

What questions would you like to ask about the process of making disciples?

In what areas would you like to improve as a disciple-maker?

We are called to make disciples of Jesus Christ—to play a part in developing people who think like Jesus, act like Jesus, and love like Jesus.

In Matthew 28 and throughout the New Testament, our mission is clear. We are called to make disciples of Jesus Christ—to play a part in developing people who think like Jesus, act like Jesus, and love like Jesus. This is our great work in the world, even as we strive to think, act, and love like Jesus in our own lives.

ENGAGE

We are commanded to make disciples. That's our mission. But what does that phrase actually mean? How do we go about the process of making disciples? Take a few moments to address those questions as a group.

Gather in smaller groups of two or three to discuss the following questions. Be open to sharing both your life experiences and your thoughts on what you've learned throughout this resource.

What have been the major landmarks in your development as a disciple of Jesus?

Who has been influential in your growth as a disciple?

What obstacles have hindered your growth as a disciple?

How would you describe your current plan for making disciples?

PRAYER REQUESTS

....

....

....

....

....

....

....

....

....

....

1. "John F. Kennedy Moon Speech," 12 September 1962 [accessed 13 May 2015]. Available from the Internet: *er.jsc.nasa.gov/seh/ricetalk.htm.*
2. Congress, House of Representatives, Committee on Science and Astronautics (1973). 1974 NASA Authorization Hearings (Hearing on H.R. 4567). Washington, D.C.: 93rd Congress, first session. OCLC 23229007.

In addition to studying God's Word, work with your group leader to create a plan for personal study, worship, and application between now and the next session. Select from the following optional activities to match your personal preferences and available time.

⬆ Worship

☑ Read your Bible. Complete the reading plan on page 154.

☐ Connect with God each day through prayer.

☐ Spend time with God by engaging the devotional experience on page 155.

➡⬅ Personal Study

☐ Read and interact with "Three Important Participles" on page 156.

☐ Read and interact with "Five Critical Commissions" on page 158.

⬅➡ Application

☐ Continue to pray daily for friends, family members, and acquaintances in your sphere of influence who are not yet disciples of Jesus. Pray for each person by name.

☐ Make sure your efforts to make disciples are fueled by Jesus' presence and authority. Set aside at least an hour this week to spend in God's presence through prayer and meditation on His Word.

☐ Commit to sharing the gospel message with at least one person this week.

☐ Memorize Acts 1:8: "But you will receive power when the Holy Spirit has come on you, and you will be my witnesses in Jerusalem, in all Judea and Samaria, and to the end of the earth."

☐ Other:

 **WORSHIP**

READING PLAN

Continue exploring the Book of Acts throughout this week. Use the space provided to record your thoughts and responses as you read.

Day 1
Acts 18:1-28

Day 2
Acts 19:1-20

Day 3
Acts 19:21-41

Day 4
Acts 20:1-38

Day 5
Acts 21:1-40

Day 6
Acts 22:1-30

Day 7
Acts 23:1-35

VINES AND BRANCHES

The Great Commission is not a suggestion. It's a command. It's Jesus sending out His disciples for a specific mission and purpose. And yet it's a command that contains an important promise: "And remember, I am with you always, to the end of the age" (Matt. 28:20).

Certainly, we should receive comfort from the promise of Jesus' presence. Yet, we will struggle in carrying out our mission if we think of Jesus' presence as an added bonus or a supplement to our own abilities. The truth is, we cannot do anything productive outside of Jesus' presence and power. We are entirely dependent on Him even as we carry out His mission.

Jesus spoke about this reality in the Gospel of John:

> 4 Remain in me, and I in you. Just as a branch is unable to produce fruit by itself unless it remains on the vine, neither can you unless you remain in me.
>
> 5 I am the vine; you are the branches. The one who remains in me and I in him produces much fruit, because you can do nothing without me. 6 If anyone does not remain in me, he is thrown aside like a branch and he withers. They gather them, throw them into the fire, and they are burned. 7 If you remain in me and my words remain in you, ask whatever you want and it will be done for you. 8 My Father is glorified by this: that you produce much fruit and prove to be my disciples.
> JOHN 15:4-8

How do you actively seek Jesus' presence each day?

What disciplines or practices help you become more aware of (and more reliant on) Jesus' presence?

THREE IMPORTANT PARTICIPLES

One of the amazing characteristics of the Bible is that the deeper you dig into the text, the more you will find and the more profoundly you will be changed. The Scriptures are a bottomless well constantly flowing with the water of life. With that in mind, we can glean some more information about the Great Commission when we take a closer look at the structure of the text itself—specifically verses 18-20:

> [18] Jesus came near and said to them, "All authority has been given to me in heaven and on earth. [19] Go, therefore, and make disciples of all nations, baptizing them in the name of the Father and of the Son and of the Holy Spirit, [20] teaching them to observe everything I have commanded you. And remember, I am with you always, to the end of the age."
> MATTHEW 28:18-20

The Great Commission is essentially a single command surrounded by three participles. In case you're not familiar with that term, a participle is a verb used to modify another element in a sentence. "Going" (or "go"), "baptizing," and "teaching" are the three participles contained in the Great Commission. Each one offers a helpful explanation of Jesus' command to "make disciples."

Going. Without being too technical, the word "go" found in modern English Bibles wasn't structured as a command in the original Greek language of the New Testament. Instead, the term was written as a participle that means "in your going" or "after you have gone." This term is directly connected to the focal point of the sentence, which is "make disciples."

In other words, "going" is a necessary element of making disciples. We can't help others encounter Jesus until we direct our focus outward, away from ourselves. Disciples of Jesus follow His example by going—across the street, across the city, across the country, and across the world—in order to show and share the good news.

What opportunities do you have to "go" on Jesus' behalf in your local church and community?

What opportunities do you have to "go" across the world?

Baptizing. The practice of baptism takes place after salvation as an illustration of what happens when we become disciples of Jesus. In that moment of conversion, we join with Jesus in both His death and His resurrection—we die to our old selves and begin a new life for Christ and His kingdom.

Baptism is more than a symbol, however. It also serves as a public declaration of allegiance to Christ—a declaration Jesus commanded us to take in the Great Commission. Therefore, when we encourage new disciples to be baptized, we are encouraging a strong first step of obedience on their journey as followers of Jesus.

> *What action steps come to mind when you think about the importance of baptism?*

Teaching. The final participle is "teaching," which involves both intellectual instruction and practical training. If Jesus had commanded us only to teach new disciples everything He commanded us, we would be free to focus solely on the doctrines of the Christian faith. We could preach and teach about justification, sanctification, the Trinity, the fall, and much more—all without the burden of having to actually do anything.

But Jesus commanded us to make disciples by "teaching them *to observe* everything I have commanded you" (v. 20, emphasis added). We've been commanded not just to teach disciples about the practices of the Christian faith, but also to model those practices. We have a duty to help disciples of Jesus—ourselves included—learn how to take action based on what we've been taught.

> *Who has been influential in teaching you about Christian principles and practices?*

> *Who has been influential in showing you how to incorporate those principles and practices in your everyday life?*

Jesus accomplished His mission on earth. Thankfully, He goes with us as we seek to make disciples for His glory and in obedience to His command.

FIVE CRITICAL COMMISSIONS

We've seen that the Great Commission in Matthew 28:19-20 serves as a helpful summary of our mission as disciples of Jesus. But it's not the only helpful summary. In fact, there are five commissions recorded in the early portions of the New Testament—all given by Jesus to His disciples.

All five commissions are worth exploring. Review the four additional commissions outlined in the following Scripture passages, beginning with the Book of Mark:

> [14] Later he appeared to the Eleven themselves as they were reclining at the table. He rebuked their unbelief and hardness of heart, because they did not believe those who saw him after he had risen. [15] Then he said to them, "Go into all the world and preach the gospel to all creation. [16] Whoever believes and is baptized will be saved, but whoever does not believe will be condemned."
> MARK 16:14-16

What are your initial impressions of these verses?

How do these verses compare and contrast with the Great Commission?

Next comes Jesus' commission near the end of Luke's Gospel, although these verses serve primarily as a reminder for the disciples to carry out everything Jesus had already said:

> [45] Then he opened their minds to understand the Scriptures. [46] He also said to them, "This is what is written: The Messiah would suffer and rise from the dead the third day, [47] and repentance for forgiveness of sins would be proclaimed in his name to all the nations, beginning at Jerusalem. [48] You are witnesses of these things. [49] And look, I am sending you what my Father promised. As for you, stay in the city until you are empowered from on high."
> LUKE 24:45-49

Jesus "opened their minds to understand the Scriptures" (v. 45).
How has the Bible guided your mission as a disciple of Jesus?

In Luke 24, Jesus made reference to sending "what my Father promised," meaning the Holy Spirit. The final chapter of John's Gospel also highlights the Spirit's role in empowering our mission:

21 Jesus said to them again, "Peace to you. As the Father has sent me, I also send you." 22 After saying this, he breathed on them and said, "Receive the Holy Spirit. 23 If you forgive the sins of any, they are forgiven them; if you retain the sins of any, they are retained."
JOHN 20:21-23

How has the Holy Spirit fueled your efforts to serve Jesus?

Finally, the first chapter in the Book of Acts contains Jesus' final words to His disciples before His ascension into heaven:

7 He said to them, "It is not for you to know times or periods that the Father has set by his own authority. 8 But you will receive power when the Holy Spirit has come on you, and you will be my witnesses in Jerusalem, in all Judea and Samaria, and to the end of the earth."
ACTS 1:7-8

What obstacles are currently hindering the gospel message from being fully proclaimed "to the end of the earth"?

What action steps will you take in the coming weeks based on your contemplation of these passages?

WE GO TOGETHER WITH CHRIST

Jesus sends us out as a community of disciples in order to make disciples.

REFLECT

In the previous session, we took a deeper look at our mission to make disciples as individual followers of Jesus. We saw that making disciples is a command, not a suggestion. And we learned that the process of disciple-making involves going out into the world, baptizing those who encounter Christ, and teaching them how to practice the fundamental truths of God's Word.

In this session, we'll explore what it means to make disciples, not only as individuals but also as a corporate body of Christ.

Which of the assignments did you explore this week? How did it go?

What did you learn or experience while reading the Bible?

What questions would you like to ask?

PRAY

Stop for a moment to pray, either individually or as a group:

- Thank God for making you part of a community within the body of Christ.

- Ask the Father to help you maintain a connection with Jesus as the Head of that body.

- Affirm your desire to join with the full body of Christ in order to engage His mission of making disciples.

INTRODUCTION

You may have noticed that visiting the doctor involves a predictable routine—especially at the beginning of the appointment. Most physicians begin by seeking to answer the same series of questions in order to get a broad assessment of your physical health:

- How tall are you?
- How much do you weigh?
- What's your blood pressure?
- Do you have any allergies?
- Do you smoke?
- Are you currently taking any prescription medications?
- Are you currently experiencing pain or discomfort?

Through hundreds of years of study, the medical profession has developed certain baseline measurements and acceptable criteria that help doctors perceive when a body may be out of alignment. The human body is intricately designed and amazingly complex, yet answering a few relatively simple questions can reveal a great deal of information about a person's overall health.

During what periods of your life have you felt the most healthy or health-conscious?

What are some important steps for promoting physical health?

Throughout the New Testament, the worldwide church is described as "the body of Christ" (see 1 Cor. 12:27, for example). Every individual disciple of Jesus has been included in that body, along with every local church and congregation. Jesus Himself governs and directs the church as its Head.

Interestingly, in the same way that a few basic questions can help evaluate a physical body, there are key factors that help us evaluate the health and productivity of the church as the body of Christ. As we'll see in this session, we know the church is healthy when disciples of Jesus work together in a corporate effort to obey Him and make more disciples.

KNOW THE STORY

The concept of the church existing as the body of Christ can be found throughout the New Testament. However, the writings of the apostle Paul offer the deepest and most direct references to that idea—including both how we should understand the body and why it's important for us to do so.

The following passage from 1 Corinthians is a helpful example of Paul's views on the body of Christ. As you read, pay attention to the strength and confidence of his words.

12 For just as the body is one and has many parts, and all the parts of that body, though many, are one body—so also is Christ. 13 For we were all baptized by one Spirit into one body—whether Jews or Greeks, whether slaves or free—and we were all given one Spirit to drink. 14 Indeed, the body is not one part but many. 15 If the foot should say, "Because I'm not a hand, I don't belong to the body," it is not for that reason any less a part of the body. 16 And if the ear should say, "Because I'm not an eye, I don't belong to the body," it is not for that reason any less a part of the body. 17 If the whole body were an eye, where would the hearing be? If the whole body were an ear, where would the sense of smell be? 18 But as it is, God has arranged each one of the parts in the body just as he wanted. 19 And if they were all the same part, where would the body be? 20 As it is, there are many parts, but one body. ...

27 Now you are the body of Christ, and individual members of it.
1 CORINTHIANS 12:12-20,27

How would you summarize the different principles Paul communicated in these verses?

Why is it important for all disciples of Jesus to understand and apply these verses?

As usual, Paul didn't mince words when he wrote the above passage. He spoke clearly and confidently. The church is the body of Christ. All disciples are included in that body. Therefore, all disciples have important work to do.

UNPACK THE STORY

WE ARE THE BODY OF CHRIST

One of the more interesting implications of Paul's teaching in 1 Corinthians 12 is that there's no such thing as an isolated disciple of Jesus. It's become popular in recent years for people to proclaim their intention to follow Jesus without connecting themselves to the broader church. According to Paul, however, such a concept is impossible.

To be a disciple of Jesus is to be intricately and intimately involved in the church. The moment we experience salvation, we are grafted into the body of Christ as one more of its "many parts" (v. 12).

How would you describe your experiences with the church over the course of your life?

> Not only are you connected with Jesus as part of His body, but you are also positioned in just the right way to accomplish the work to which God has called you.

You are part of the body of Christ, and that is wonderful news. Because even with the church's past mistakes and current faults, Jesus is the Head. You are a part of *His* body, which means you are intimately connected to Him.

Notice this additional promise from God's Word: "But as it is, God has arranged each one of the parts in the body *just as he wanted*" (1 Cor. 12:18, emphasis added). Not only are you connected with Jesus as part of His body, but you are also positioned in just the right way to accomplish the work to which God has called you.

You have been specifically and specially designed to serve Jesus as a working member of His body.

Many Christians feel uncertain or unsettled about their place in their local church, which is understandable given that people—even well-meaning disciples of Christ—aren't perfect. Still, Jesus has promised us a place in His body. Therefore, our service in the church becomes a matter of faith more than comfort.

In what ways has God equipped you to serve the church?

WE WORK TOGETHER TO MAKE DISCIPLES

There's no question that being part of the church—both in local congregations and smaller groups—provides a number of benefits. We can find community and friendship in the church, for example. We can find support and encouragement. We can find education and transformational teaching. All of these are wonderful blessings.

But we must always remember that the body of Christ wasn't designed solely to bless the members of that body. Rather, the church exists to accomplish the will of its Head, which is Christ. And it is Christ's will for the church to make disciples.

Look back to the early church, for example:

> [41] So those who accepted his message were baptized, and that day about three thousand people were added to them. [42] They devoted themselves to the apostles' teaching, to the fellowship, to the breaking of bread, and to prayer.
>
> [43] Everyone was filled with awe, and many wonders and signs were being performed through the apostles. [44] Now all the believers were together and held all things in common. [45] They sold their possessions and property and distributed the proceeds to all, as any had need. [46] Every day they devoted themselves to meeting together in the temple, and broke bread from house to house. They ate their food with joyful and sincere hearts, [47] praising God and enjoying the favor of all the people. Every day the Lord added to their number those who were being saved.
> ACTS 2:41-47

The church exists to accomplish the will of its Head, which is Christ. And it is Christ's will for the church to make disciples.

How do these verses show obedience to the Great Commission?

What are some of the practical ways your group or congregation works toward obeying the Great Commission?

How has the Holy Spirit been leading you to participate in the work of your church?

ENGAGE

It's not always easy for people to work well with others. Even among disciples of Jesus, it can be difficult to set aside our own egos and agendas in order to function as a team. For that reason, it's important for the members of your group to be intentional about finding ways to strive for unity together.

Fortunately, one of the simplest methods for strengthening the bonds within your group is also one of the most effective. That method is prayer. When you and your group members join together to intercede for one another in the presence of God's Spirit, you will experience greater unity. You will develop deeper levels of trust, encouragement, and appreciation.

As a group, spend several minutes sharing about issues or circumstances for which you'd like prayer.

Pray for one another out loud. As each group member prays, the others should focus on mentally echoing his or her statements to God.

Conclude by committing to pray daily for one another by name until the next group gathering.

PRAYER REQUESTS

....

....

....

....

....

....

....

....

....

....

In addition to studying God's Word, work with your group leader to create a plan for personal study, worship, and application between now and the next session. Select from the following optional activities to match your personal preferences and available time.

⬆ Worship

☑ Read your Bible. Complete the reading plan on page 168.

☐ Connect with God each day through prayer.

☐ Spend time with God by engaging the devotional experience on page 169.

➡⬅ Personal Study

☐ Read and interact with "Find Your Place in the Body" on page 170.

☐ Read and interact with "Join the Body in Making Disciples" on page 172.

⬅➡ Application

☐ Take out your calendar and review your current involvement with your local church. Are you fully investing yourself as a functioning member of the body of Christ?

☐ Memorize Colossians 1:17-18: "He is before all things, and by him all things hold together. He is also the head of the body, the church; he is the beginning, the firstborn from the dead, so that he might come to have first place in everything."

☐ Identify a church function or group encounter in the near future to which you can invite friends or family members who need to meet Jesus. Pray for these individuals each day, and be alert for opportunities to make the invitation.

☐ Invite a fellow disciple to join you in a spiritual activity—studying God's Word, memorizing Scripture, prayer, evangelism, fasting, and so on.

☐ Other:

 **WORSHIP**

READING PLAN

Conclude your reading of the Book of Acts this week. Use the space provided to record your thoughts and responses as you read.

Day 1
Acts 24:1-27

Day 2
Acts 25:1-27

Day 3
Acts 26:1-23

Day 4
Acts 26:24-32

Day 5
Acts 27:1-44

Day 6
Acts 28:1-16

Day 7
Acts 28:17-31

CONTENTMENT IN THE BODY

To be included in the body of Christ is a wonderful privilege. We have the chance to serve God even as we enjoy the benefits of community within the church. Yet, there are still obstacles that need to be overcome. There are still areas of sin or misunderstanding that can cause pain for individuals and friction within the church.

One of those obstacles is the presence of discontentment. To be frank, it's common for disciples of Jesus to feel dissatisfied about their roles within the church. Sometimes this is a mild desire for more recognition, more influence, or less stressful responsibilities. Other times our discontentment becomes a full-fledged root of bitterness and pride.

In either case, the apostle Paul was clear that a lack of contentment will have dangerous consequences within the body of Christ:

> 12 For just as the body is one and has many parts, and all the parts of that body, though many, are one body—so also is Christ. ...
>
> 21 The eye cannot say to the hand, "I don't need you!" Or again, the head can't say to the feet, "I don't need you!" 22 On the contrary, those parts of the body that are weaker are indispensable. 23 And those parts of the body that we consider less honorable, we clothe these with greater honor, and our unrespectable parts are treated with greater respect, 24 which our respectable parts do not need. Instead, God has put the body together, giving greater honor to the less honorable, 25 so that there would be no division in the body, but that the members would have the same concern for each other. 26 So if one member suffers, all the members suffer with it; if one member is honored, all the members rejoice with it.
> 1 CORINTHIANS 12:12,21-26

Do you feel content with your role in the body of Christ? Explain.

What disciplines or practices can help you increase your level of contentment as a disciple of Jesus?

FIND YOUR PLACE IN THE BODY

If you've been transformed as a disciple of Jesus Christ, then you are part of His body, the church. Even more, you have a specific role and function as a member of that body—you've been uniquely designed and specially placed to advance the work of the broader church within the community of your local group and congregation.

Therefore, one of the best ways to make sure you're contributing well is to identify your role and function within your church. In what ways have you been gifted? How can you contribute to the life and ministry of your church community? These are questions you've been pondering throughout this session. Thankfully, the apostle Paul highlighted several important roles within the church during his letter to the Christians in Ephesus:

> 11 And he himself gave some to be apostles, some prophets, some evangelists, some pastors and teachers, 12 equipping the saints for the work of ministry, to build up the body of Christ, 13 until we all reach unity in the faith and in the knowledge of God's Son, growing into maturity with a stature measured by Christ's fullness. 14 Then we will no longer be little children, tossed by the waves and blown around by every wind of teaching, by human cunning with cleverness in the techniques of deceit. 15 But speaking the truth in love, let us grow in every way into him who is the head—Christ. 16 From him the whole body, fitted and knit together by every supporting ligament, promotes the growth of the body for building up itself in love by the proper working of each individual part.
> EPHESIANS 4:11-16

What are the roles and functions within the body of Christ mentioned in the above passage?

What are some additional roles and functions carried out by members of your church today?

Notice Paul's emphasis in verse 16 that the body is built up and remains healthy through "the proper working of each individual part." That's you. Every disciple of Jesus has a share in maintaining the health and productivity of the church. More, we have a responsibility to do our part in helping the body of Christ fulfill its mission—a responsibility that includes consequences when we neglect our duty.

Jesus made that clear when He shared the parable of the talents with His disciples.

> *Read Matthew 25:14-30. How would you summarize the primary theme of Jesus' parable?*

> *What are some recent ways you've invested your talents—your gifts and abilities—in order to make disciples within the body of Christ?*

Many people feel hesitant about pouring themselves into the church's mission to make disciples, and there are many reasons for that hesitation. Some simply don't want to give up greater control of their lives. Others aren't willing to let go of cherished possessions or long-held habits. Still, others feel they don't possess the right gifts for making disciples—they don't have the gift of teaching or they don't possess a striking personal testimony.

In the end, all of these excuses boil down to the same thing: disobedience. Our Master has commanded us to work together as His body in order to make disciples for His kingdom. That is our mission.

What you do next is your choice.

> *How would you describe your specific role within the body of Christ?*

> *What obstacles are currently hindering you from engaging that role to a greater degree?*

JOIN THE BODY IN MAKING DISCIPLES

Jesus came to our world with a mission to redeem our world—us included. He became one of us so that He could teach us and model what it means to follow God. He suffered on our behalf. He died as the atonement for our sins. And His glorious resurrection made it possible for all people to join with Him in a new and restored relationship with God. That was His mission, and He accomplished it.

Jesus gave His disciples a mission as well—one that should drive us each day to expand His kingdom and bring glory to God. Take another look at the mission as He expressed it:

> [18] Jesus came near and said to them, "All authority has been given to me in heaven and on earth. [19] Go, therefore, and make disciples of all nations, baptizing them in the name of the Father and of the Son and of the Holy Spirit, [20] teaching them to observe everything I have commanded you. And remember, I am with you always, to the end of the age."
> MATTHEW 28:18-20

How has your understanding of these verses changed or deepened in recent weeks?

In what ways have you actively obeyed Jesus' command to make disciples in recent months?

"Make disciples." That's your mission as an individual follower of Jesus. Yet, you cannot accomplish that mission alone. You need to work as part of the body of Christ if you want to make any progress—let alone make disciples. You need to actively plug yourself into the life of your local church.

With that in mind, use the following assessments and questions to help you continue moving forward in obedience to God and to demonstrate active passion for your mission as a disciple of Christ.

How confident do you feel in your ability to make disciples?

1	2	3	4	5	6	7	8	9	10
Not confident									Very confident